CHARACTER-EDUCATION STORIES

Character-Education Lessons

Including

Stories, Poems,

Discussion Questions,

&

Activities

For

Elementary Students

ILLUSTRATED BY
MARIE GARAFANO

CONTENTS

CHARACTER-TRAIT STORIES FOR THE HOLIDAYS 217

INTRODUCTION

Character-Education Stories is a compilation of 32 stories and poems, with character-education themes, written by many different authors. The stories are intended for use in any classroom, small-group, or individual situation in which the leader is teaching the particular character trait emphasized in the story.

The book is divided into three sections:

- Character-Trait Stories Emphasizing Personal Improvement

- Character-Trait Stories Emphasizing Relationships With Others

- Character-Trait Stories For Holidays (Some of these pieces were originally published in PIC (Practical Ideas for Counselors).

Each of the stories and its accompanying questions and follow-up activities has been designed to be completed in 30-40 minutes. Some stories will be more appropriate for younger elementary students, others for older elementary students. Since student populations are different, each leader must decide upon the story or poem's suitability for the grade level to which it will be presented.

HOW TO USE
CHARACTER-EDUCATION STORIES

INTRODUCING THE LESSON: The leader may introduce the story or poem by explaining how it relates to the character traits following its title. Or the leader may just read the story or poem and, when finished, have the students identify the character traits within the text.

READING THE STORY: Because the stories and poems are laid out so they may easily be reproduced, the leader may read from the book or from a reproduced copy. The leader may choose to reproduce the story for one or more students to read aloud.

DISCUSSION QUESTIONS: Most stories and poems are followed by discussion questions. Only a very few have the questions interspersed in the text and should be read by the leader, rather than the students. Suggested answers can be found in the parentheses following each question. Using these questions will allow the leader to monitor students' understanding of what's being read. The leader should feel free to add or delete for the benefit of specific student groups.

FOLLOW-UP ACTIVITIES: Follow-up activities are included for the purpose of concluding the lesson. Some require reproducing activity sheets. Others are interactive. Before beginning any lesson, check to see which activities will be used and what materials are necessary.

CHARACTER-EDUCATION STORIES

CHARACTER-TRAIT STORIES EMPHASIZING PERSONAL IMPROVEMENT

WIRE AND STRING
GRADES 3-5

BULLYING
SELF-ESTEEM
TOLERANCE

WRITTEN BY BETSY DAVIDSON

Betsy Davidson lives in New Mexico. She is also the author of *Twyla Tulip And Her Talking Toes,* published by Mar*co Products.

Note: Throughout the story are places for the reader to stop and ask the students questions. These are self-insight questions, and the leader should accept any appropriate answers.

WIRE AND STRING

Somewhere back in the country, there were two little boys who were very confused. The first little boy was light-skinned, with freckles and blond hair that just kind of swung loose. He was poor and wore ragged clothes and always looked like he needed a haircut. Some of the children at school sometimes made fun of him. This boy's name was Timmy.

The second little boy had very dark skin and black curly hair. He, too, came from a family with very little money. Some children at school made fun of him, too, because his skin was a different color than theirs and his clothes were old. This boy's name was Kenny.

Timmy and Kenny were often sad because some of the other children were so mean to them.

There was also a lonely old man who lived not far from a small pond surrounded by trees. The old man had been in a terrible accident years before, and one side of his face was so scarred that some people did not want to look at him. Others made fun of him. But those who truly knew this man knew that he was kind and gentle. Oddly enough, both boys' grandparents had known this man well and both boys had heard their parents describe him as one of the kindest and gentlest persons one would ever want to know. Neither of the boys had ever seen the old man, although they had both heard of him and they both knew his name was Dave.

Each boy had a place—a secret place. Each boy had made his own fishing pole out of branches and twine. Each of them would go down to his secret place—a little pond in the middle of some large trees—and feel a sense of peace because they were away from the children who were mean to them. Timmy and Kenny didn't know each other. Then one day they both went to their secret place at the same time and bumped right into one another.

"What are you doing here?" Timmy asked the dark-skinned boy. "What do you mean? This is my secret place," Kenny replied. "But ... this is *my* secret place," answered Timmy. Even though the boys were shocked to realize they both had the same secret place, it was kind of nice to know that they had someone with whom to share their secret.

"Let's promise each other that neither of us will ever tell anyone about this place," suggested Kenny. "Great idea!" Timmy agreed and they made a pact. Then Kenny said, "Wow! Your hair sure is stringy. I'm going to call you String." "Well," replied

Timmy, "your hair looks like wire. Look! When I touch it, it pops right back. I'm going to call you Wire." And so the boys got their nicknames, Wire and String.

STOP! Ask the students: Do any of you if have nicknames? If you do, how do you believe you got them?

Wire had been having a really bad time and didn't go to his secret place for a whole week. The bullies had been exceptionally mean to him all week. But today was Saturday, and he didn't have to go to school. Wire felt good about that, so he took his fishing pole and walked to his secret pond. Once he got there, he started thinking about the mean things some of the children had said to him. He started to cry.

Then he heard a noise, like some kind of music. He looked up and saw an old, old man walking toward him and playing a harmonica. As the man got closer, Wire noticed a horrible scar on one side of his face. He stopped crying and just stared at the man's scar. He knew who the man was because he had heard his parents talk of him. Wire knew this was a good man, but he couldn't help being horrified by the man's face. Then the old man said:

> *"Don't be frightened! I'm on your side.*
> *I'm here to help, so please don't hide.*
> *I want to take away all that sadness*
> *And replace it with a lot of gladness."*

Wire got scared, dropped his fishing pole, and ran all the way home. He didn't tell anyone about meeting the old man, partly because he was ashamed of the way he had behaved. He felt a little guilty for being afraid of something as silly as the way another person looks. He didn't know when he would go back to his secret place, but he hoped he would have the courage to face the old man again.

STOP! Ask the students: Why would Wire would need courage to face the old man again?

String had had a really bad week, too. It just seemed like some of the children at school got meaner and meaner with their ugly name-calling and their ugly behavior. He took his fishing pole that same Saturday and went to the secret place. When he saw Wire's pole, he worried that something might have happened to his friend. Then he looked around and saw the old man standing there. Just as Wire had, String stared at the old man's scarred face. He knew he shouldn't be frightened by the man, because he had heard about him. But he'd never seen anyone who looked like that. When the old man saw String, he stopped playing his harmonica and said:

> *"Don't be frightened! I'm on your side.*
> *I'm here to help, so please don't hide.*
> *I want to take away all that sadness*
> *And replace it with a lot of gladness."*

String listened and stood with his mouth open for a good two minutes. Then he simply turned around and walked home. He wasn't really afraid, because he'd heard only good things about this man from his parents. But this was the first time he'd actually seen him, and he just couldn't bear to look at a face like that. String didn't tell anyone he had seen the man, but he knew he wanted to return to the place where they had met.

STOP! Ask the students: Why do you think String did not tell anyone about meeting the old man?

Another week went by. Wire and String went to school and many of the other children teased them. They teased String because of his ragged clothes and stringy hair. They teased Wire because of his color, his clothes, and his hair. On Saturday morning, Wire decided to be brave and go to his secret fishing pond. He hoped his fishing pole would still be there. He dug up some worms and walked down to his private hideaway, promising himself nothing was going to make him run away. He saw his pole, sat on the ground next to it, and sure enough, the old man with the scarred face came walking toward him. When he was close enough, he said:

> *"Hello, Son! Please be brave.*
> *I'd like for you to call me Dave.*
> *I'd like to say you're a fine-looking boy.*
> *Please don't be afraid and don't be coy.*
> *I want you to see how special you are,*
> *As beautiful as a shining star!*
> *You have the prettiest, darkest skin,*
> *To not be proud would be a sin.*
> *In your teeth, it brings out the whiteness.*
> *In your eyes, it brings out the brightness.*
> *Those big brown eyes say so much,*
> *And that wiry hair is fun to touch!*
> *So about your color, you should always be proud.*
> *And don't be afraid to shout it out loud."*

Wire smiled from ear to ear, showing his bright white teeth and the glow in his big brown eyes. He felt good about himself now and couldn't stop smiling. The old man turned around and walked away, quietly playing his harmonica. Wire couldn't help noticing how well the old man played the harmonica and how nice his voice sounded when he spoke. He realized that when he took the time to look beyond the ugly part of the old man's face, he could see only kindness and caring in his expression.

Wire sat for a few hours more, thinking and catching a few fish. Then he got up and whistled all the way home. He was glad he hadn't run away again. He just wished that some of the children at school would look at his good qualities and stop being so mean to him. When he got home, he told his parents about his meeting with the old man. They were glad that their son had been able to talk with the old man. Wire didn't tell anyone else about the meeting, because anyone he told would know about his secret place.

STOP! Ask the students: Why do people often judge others only by how they look on the outside?

String didn't feel ready to go back to the secret place until Sunday. When he got there, he saw the old man walking toward him, as Wire had seen the day before. He didn't feel the way he had felt the first time he'd seen the old man. String was so sad for himself because of the way his feelings had been hurt, that he just started to hope he hadn't hurt the old man's feelings when he couldn't stand looking at his scarred face. Then he heard the old man say:

> *"Hello, Son! Don't be sad.*
> *Things aren't really all that bad.*
> *You have a family who love and adore you,*
> *And a lot of people who like you, too.*
> *Your clothes may not be pretty, but they're always clean.*
> *Just don't pay attention to those who are mean.*
> *Your freckles are cute, and I love your hair.*
> *That beautiful color is rather rare.*
> *You're a fine-looking boy with beautiful eyes.*
> *But more importantly, you're very wise.*
> *So be my friend and please be brave.*
> *And by the way, you can call me Dave."*

Then Dave turned around and, playing his harmonica, disappeared into the bushes.

String felt a lot better. He needed a friend like Dave. He stayed at the pond awhile, and although he didn't catch anything, he went home with a smile on his face. He felt better about himself because of what the man said about him and because he had been able to see beyond the man's scarred face. When String told his parents about meeting the old man, they were happy that he had learned to see beyond looks, handicaps, or anything that is superficial. Their son had learned that we can all learn from one another.

STOP! Ask the students to name one thing they could teach the other students in the class that they might not already know how to do.

Wire couldn't wait to get back to his secret place! When Friday came and he had a free afternoon, he ran to the fishing pond. He was hoping to see Dave again and ask him some questions. After waiting awhile, he heard the harmonica in the distance, coming closer and closer. When they were within hearing distance of each other, Wire looked up and said, "Hey Dave! What's happening?" Dave answered:

> *"Hello, Son! You're looking blue.*
> *Tell me, please, what's troubling you."*

Wire poured his heart out. He told Dave about all the mean children who made fun of him and called him nasty, ugly names because of his color, his clothes, and his hair. He told Dave how he felt so bad that he never wanted to go back to school. Dave listened. Then said:

> *"Only unhappy people are mean.*
> *It acts like a shield or a kind of a screen*
> *To hide all the sorrow they are feeling.*
> *It isn't right, but it's their way of dealing*

With all the turmoil going on inside
That they are desperately trying to hide.

"So don't be hurt by what they say.
Try to realize that it's just their way
Of hiding all the terrible pain
Going on inside their brains.
So when they make fun of your hair or shirt,
Don't get offended and don't be hurt.

"When they make fun of the color of your skin,
There is a sure way you can win.
Smile at them and don't be sad.
They're the ones who are being bad.

"Never let them see your fears.
Never let them see your tears.
If you don't cry or moan or groan,
Sooner or later, they'll leave you alone!"

Then the old man turned around. Playing his harmonica, he disappeared into the bushes.

Wire felt a lot better. He actually started feeling sorry for those mean children. He stayed for a while, then went home thankful for his loving family and thankful for having met Dave. All of a sudden, he realized that when he looked at Dave, he wasn't thinking about his face any more.

STOP! Ask the students: What advice did Dave give to Wire about how to handle the bullies?

String didn't get back to his secret place until Saturday. Shortly after he arrived, he heard the harmonica. String looked up and saw Dave walking toward him. Soon he, like Wire, was telling Dave about the other children making fun of his clothes, his hair, and even his family. Dave listened, then replied:

"I want you to try to understand fully
That when a child becomes a bully,
It's usually due to an unhappy life
Filled with turmoil and filled with strife.
A child who is mean and nasty and bad
Is a child who within is very sad.
A child who gets pleasure from calling you names
Is a child who is playing dangerous games.

"You can only feel sorry for a child like that.
So instead of thinking that child is a brat,
Realize how unhappy that child must be
When meanness is all that child can see.
Now there's something else I'd like to mention
When bullies start to bother you, don't pay attention.
Smile at them and don't be sad.
They're the ones who are being bad.

Never let them see your fears.
Never let them see your tears.
If you don't cry or moan or groan,
Sooner or later, they'll leave you alone!"

Then the old man turned around and walked into the bushes. He was playing his harmonica.

String sat there realizing everything that he had heard was true. He decided, then and there, that he'd never again be saddened or hurt by unkind words that came from others. He realized that they were the ones who were truly unhappy. Then he packed up his things and headed home. He was thankful for his happy home and thankful for having met Dave.

STOP! Ask the students: What did String learn about bullies from Dave?

The school year was almost over for Wire and String. Summer vacation was only three weeks away. For the first of those three weeks, Wire and String did exactly what Dave had told them to do. And it worked! At the end of the first week, Wire and String bumped into each other and made plans to go their secret place on Saturday. Neither of them said anything about meeting Dave.

On Saturday, as String and Wire were walking to their secret place, they passed two big bullies. When the bullies started to make fun of them, Wire and String just smiled and acted as friendly as they could. The bullies walked away. Wire and String looked at each other and put their arms around one another. From that moment on, they became the best of friends. When they arrived at their secret place, they threw their fishing lines into the water and sat there and talked. Neither of them mentioned Dave. When they went home, they made plans to go fishing the following Sunday. But they still did not mention Dave.

STOP! Ask the students: Why do you think the boys did not tell each other that they had met Dave?

When String went back to school on Monday, the bullies ganged up on him. They started teasing him because some of them had seen him with Wire. Now they not only called him names, but they also said some really mean things about Wire. String tried to ignore them, but it was hard to do. It was a long time before he was able to walk away from the bullies and go home. After this awful day, he wanted to get away to his secret place.

Once he was there, he started to think about Dave and about how much he wanted to see the old man. Suddenly he heard the harmonica! When Dave had come near enough, words of sadness burst from String. String told Dave how mean the children were and that they were making fun of Wire. In fact, he told Dave that he was more afraid for Wire than for himself. Dave listened and reassured String that Wire would be all right, that bullies don't have any true friends, and that he should just continue acting as he had told him to before. Then he left, telling String that he would not be back.

Wire had the same experience. The bullies teased him and made fun of String. Wire felt the same way as String. He could take what the bullies were saying about him, but he hated it when they talked about his friend. Wire, like String, wanted to talk with Dave. He went to the secret place on Saturday morning and, like String, poured his heart out to his friend. When Wire had finished talking, Dave told him, as he had told String, to continue doing what he had done before and to always feel proud of himself. Then he left, telling Wire that he would not be back.

STOP! Ask the students: Why do you think Dave told the boys he would not be back?

On Sunday, Wire and String met to go to their secret place. "Hey! What's happening?" asked Wire. "Not much! Let's go catch some fish," answered String. They walked to their fishing hole, sat down, threw their lines into the water and looked at one another. Somehow, they both knew the other had become a friend of the old man with the scarred face. They just smiled at each other, put their arms around one another, and remained the best of friends for the rest of their lives.

And even though bullies sometimes tried to tease each of the boys, neither Wire nor String was ever bothered. They had both learned the important secrets of dealing with bullies, as well as some important secrets of life itself from their very own special friend—that old man with the scarred face, the soothing harmonica, and the kind voice. Dave.

FOLLOW-UP ACTIVITIES

1. **My Secret Place:** Distribute art paper and crayons or markers to each student. Remind the students that both Wire and String had a secret place that he went to get away from the bullies at school. Explain that you don't have to be bullied to have a secret place. You could have a secret place for any reason. Tell the students to draw a picture of a place that they think would make a good secret place. When everyone has finished, have the students share their drawings and explain the reason for their choices.

2. **Who Are You?:** Collect a large group of pictures of people from magazines. Make the pictures as varied as possible. Reproduce a copy of *Who Are You?* (page 23) for each student group. Divide the students into groups. Give each group a picture and a copy of the *Who Are You?* activity sheet. Tell the students to work together and write answers for the picture on the activity sheet. Tell the students how much time they have to complete the assignment. When the allotted time has elapsed, have the groups exchange pictures and repeat the activity. Continue the process until each group has seen four pictures. Then collect the pictures. Hold up one picture and have the groups who worked on that picture tell how they answered the questions about it. Note the similarities and differences between the answers. Continue doing this until all the pictures have been shown. Then ask the students, "Why didn't each of you come up with the same answers to the questions?" Continue the discussion until the students realize that, like Dave, a person cannot be judged by outward appearance alone.

WHO ARE YOU?

PICTURE #1

This is a picture of a _____ .

The age of the person in this picture is _____ .

Circle the character traits you believe this person to have. Do not circle any traits unless you are able to explain why you have chosen them.

patience	tolerance	caring	trustworthiness
leadership	fairness	loyalty	dependability

PICTURE #2

This is a picture of a _____ .

The age of the person in this picture is _____ .

Circle the character traits you believe this person to have. Do not circle any traits unless you are able to explain why you have chosen them.

patience	tolerance	caring	trustworthiness
leadership	fairness	loyalty	dependability

PICTURE #3

This is a picture of a _____ .

The age of the person in this picture is _____ .

Circle the character traits you believe this person to have. Do not circle any traits unless you are able to explain why you have chosen them.

patience	tolerance	caring	trustworthiness
leadership	fairness	loyalty	dependability

PICTURE #4

This is a picture of a _____ .

The age of the person in this picture is _____ .

Circle the character traits you believe this person to have. Do not circle any traits unless you are able to explain why you have chosen them.

patience	tolerance	caring	trustworthiness
leadership	fairness	loyalty	dependability

PENELOPE PROCTOR'S PROBLEM
GRADES 2-4

PROPER HYGIENE
SELF-RESPECT

WRITTEN BY WANDA S. COOK

Wanda Cook is an elementary counselor in Texas. She is a contributor to *Special Situations*, published by Mar*co Products.

PENELOPE PROCTOR'S PROBLEM

After a busy day of moving into their brand new home, Penelope Proctor and her parents enjoyed a hearty meal of crispy carrots, tender lettuce leaves, and juicy wildflowers.

Penelope Proctor was a bright and energetic little bunny. She and her family had decided to leave their old home because the animals at Penelope's school teased her and called her mean names. For the life of them, neither Penelope nor her parents could figure out why her classmates were so cruel and so unkind. Penelope only knew that the mean names made her feel sad, confused, and all alone.

"The change will do her good," Mrs. Proctor whispered to Mr. Proctor as they watched Penelope gobble up the last morsel of her tasty meal.

After dinner, the Proctors enjoyed a soothing cup of hot chamomile tea. Then the exhausted family unpacked their last box. Finally, the weary Proctors went to bed. They did not do the dishes. They did not shower, clean their teeth, or brush the tangles from their matted fur. But that wasn't unusual for Penelope or her parents. That was the way the Proctor family had always done things.

After a good night's rest, the warm and friendly sun brought the promise of a beautiful and exciting day. Penelope grabbed her backpack and matching lunch box. Then she dashed out the front door and caught the bright yellow school bus. Minutes later, the school bus stopped in front of Stephen B. O'Hare Elementary. Penelope hopped off.

Penelope's new teacher, Mrs. Cottontail, was busy writing the daily assignment on the chalkboard when Penelope hopped into the room. She greeted Penelope kindly and then introduced her to the rest of the class. "Class," said Mrs. Cottontail, tapping her pointer on her thick wooden desk. "I would like to introduce you to your new classmate. Her name is Penelope—Penelope Proctor." "Hi," the bunnies said in unison, as they waved and flashed Penelope friendly smiles.

Penelope swayed nervously from left to right. She was excited, but a little bit bashful about being in front of her new classmates. Nevertheless, Penelope waved back and flashed them a warm and friendly smile. But Penelope's smile revealed neither her excitement nor her shyness. Penelope's smile revealed chunks of carrots, pieces of lettuce leaves, and bits of wildflowers all stuck in her front teeth. They were left there from last night's dinner.

The animals could not believe their eyes. But for the sake of politeness, they pretended not to see Penelope's colorful collection. All the animals, that is except Jimmy—Jimmy Jumper. When Jimmy Jumper saw the food in Penelope's teeth, he let out a long, high-pitched squeal. He then lay his head on his desk and laughed so loudly that he fell from his seat and rolled onto the hard wooden floor. "Did … did … did you see that?" Jimmy Jumper said while laughing and struggling to catch his breath. By this time, Mrs. Cottontail had quietly made her way to Jimmy's seat. She knelt down beside him, placed her paw on his right shoulder and gave him **"the eye."** After that, Jimmy stopped his foolishness, returned to his seat, and pretended not to see the food in Penelope's teeth, just like the other animals had pretended not to see it.

The soft chime of the 9:00 bell calmed the students and invited them to start their school day. Penelope, still confused by Jimmy Jumper's strange behavior, moved quietly to her front row desk. "Jimmy Jumper is weird," Penelope thought as she sat in her seat. "But for the sake of politeness, I will pretend that he is not."

The morning was busy and lunchtime came quickly. Penelope could hardly wait to devour the crunchy turnips and tasty blueberries that her mom had packed for her lunch. She sat at a table with two other girls from her class. The friendly girls had delicious lunches, too. Suzy Primrose's mom had given her fresh-baked bread and crispy celery sticks for lunch, and Zeta Zindler's mom had given her fresh, meaty cucumbers and slices of sweet navel oranges.

The two girls traded food with each other as they had done since the first day of school. "Penelope, your berries look delicious," said Zeta. "**Don't** trade with Penelope," whispered Suzy, interrupting her. "Well, why not?" Zeta whispered back. "Penelope didn't wash her paws with soap and water before lunch, and they don't look very clean. Mrs. Cottontail said that we should always wash away the germs before eating our lunches," answered Suzy.

Penelope noticed that the girls were whispering. She also noticed that the two bunnies hadn't asked her to trade, but she thought it was because she was new at school. She had no idea that her unclean teeth and unwashed paws were already giving her a pretty "dirty" reputation.

After lunch and recess, the students returned to the classroom to begin their spelling assignment. The task for the day was to create a simple crossword puzzle using that week's spelling words. The animals worked in groups of threes. Reyna and Renee, the Flopsey twins, invited Penelope to work with them.

After a few minutes of working on the assignment, Reyna asked Mrs. Cottontail if she could speak with her privately. "What is it, Reyna?" asked Mrs. Cottontail. They went into the hall and quietly closed the classroom door behind them.

"Mrs. Cottontail," said Reyna, "it's Penelope Proctor."

"What about Penelope, Reyna?" Mrs. Cottontail asked.

"She doesn't smell like fresh flower petals," answered Reyna.

"Reyna," said Mrs. Cottontail, "you're not making any sense. Please explain what you mean."

"Well," said Reyna, "Mama told Renee and me that little bunnies should always have clean fluffy fur and should smell like the fresh flower petals she rubs behind our ears after our bath. And honestly speaking, Mrs. Cottontail, Penelope just doesn't smell that way."

After Reyna had finished speaking, Mrs. Cottontail encouraged her to go inside and finish her assignment. Mrs. Cottontail stood out in the hall and thought long and hard about what Reyna had said. She decided to pay a special visit to Mrs. Feelwell, the school nurse, after school. They decided that because it was Penelope's first day at school it was too soon to make a judgment. They decided to wait awhile and see if things got better or worse.

Days passed. Things still were not going well for Penelope. Now all of the animals were complaining about how unpleasant it was to sit near her or to work closely with her. The animals liked Penelope, and they were neither cruel nor unkind. But they always found an excuse not to be near her. Once again, just like at her old school, this bright and energetic little bunny felt sad, confused, and all alone.

Mrs. Cottontail met again with Mrs. Feelwell. They decided it was time to pay Penelope's mom a visit. So when the school day ended, Mrs. Cottontail grabbed her soft, pearl-colored shawl and made her way to 1517 Hip Hop Lane. Once there, Mrs. Cottontail walked up the long winding steps that led to the Proctor's front door. She rang the doorbell and Mrs. Proctor opened the front door.

"Good evening, Mrs. Proctor. I am Penelope's teacher, Mrs. Cottontail. May I please come in?" asked Mrs. Cottontail.

"Why, of course," replied Mrs. Proctor, flashing a broad smile just like Penelope's. "Come in. Oh, please, do come in!" And just like Penelope's broad smile, Mrs. Proctor had a colorful collection of carrots, lettuce leaves, and wildflowers stuck in her two front teeth. And for the sake of politeness, Mrs. Cottontail, like her students, pretended not to notice.

When Mrs. Cottontail entered the Proctor's home, she could not believe her eyes. The sink was overflowing with dirty dishes. There were cracked egg shells and greasy food all over the kitchen floor and walls. And the Proctor's stove was oozing a thick, sticky, yellowish slime.

"Have a seat, dear," Mrs. Proctor said rapidly. "Have a seat. Have a seat," she repeated.

"**Where?**" wondered Mrs. Cottontail, as she looked around the untidy house.

"Sit here, sit here dear," continued Mrs. Proctor pointing to an old wooden rocker.

As Mrs. Cottontail tunneled her way to the chair, she felt something squish between her two left toes. "**What** was that?" she asked in disgust as she examined the ugly green mess underneath her snow white paw.

"Just an old green tomato. Just an old tomato," answered Mrs. Proctor. "Last week's dinner. Last week's dinner, I tell you. Kick it to the side, dear, just kick it to the side."

"Mrs. Proctor," began Mrs. Cottontail, cleaning the goo from her dainty little paw. "I am here because our school nurse, Mrs. Feelwell, is sponsoring a school-wide health fair this Friday in the gymnasium. Since you are new to our school, I came to give you, Mr. Proctor, and Penelope a ***personal*** invitation."

"Thank you, dear, thank you. We'd be happy to come, happy to come," repeated Mrs. Proctor. "This Friday, you say, this Friday. We'll be there, dear. We'll be there."

After hearing all that Mrs. Cottontail had to say, Mrs. Proctor stood up, and scratched the bottom of her crumpled, bushy tail. When she had finished scratching, she burped—***deeply, long, and very loudly***. Then she escorted a very shaken Mrs. Cottontail to the front door. "Mrs. Proctor doesn't smell of fresh flower petals," thought Mrs. Cottontail as she nervously wrapped her pearl-colored shawl around her soft furry shoulders and quickly made her way down the long winding steps.

On Friday, the health fair began with Mrs. Feelwell introducing the first speaker, Dr. Hopper, a local dentist. He showed the animals how to care for their teeth and gums. He also showed them what would happen to their teeth if they didn't brush and floss. After his presentation, Dr. Hopper gave all the students and their parents toothbrushes, toothpaste, and dental floss.

The second speaker was Dr. Sniffer. She explained to the bunnies the importance of keeping their fur and paws clean, and she showed them how to do it. She gave them free soap, sponges, shampoo, and fur brushes.

The last speaker was Dr. Skipper. He taught the bunnies and their families all about germs and their dirty little hiding places. He helped them understand that germs live on unclean surfaces and that the little critters could really make them sick.

Penelope and her family listened carefully to each speaker. They could hardly believe their ears. It seemed everything they were not doing was hurting them. They didn't want this, and as soon as they returned home, they began changing things. First they scrubbed the dirty dishes. Then they cleaned the greasy garbage from the floor. When they had finished doing that, they scrubbed up all the spills on the kitchen stove and scraped the old food from the walls, just as Dr. Skipper had said they should do.

After they had finished cleaning the house, the Proctors used the soap, shampoo, and sponges that Dr. Sniffer had given them to scrub their paws and clean their fur. Mrs. Proctor even went out and gathered fresh flower petals. Finally, they used the toothbrushes, toothpaste, and floss that Dr. Hopper had given them to clean their teeth and gums.

Penelope Proctor's family learned many new and wonderful health habits at the health fair. Penelope's new clean habits allowed her to make many close friends. No longer does she feel sad and lonely. Now she feels fresh, clean, and very pretty.

Now Penelope's classmates love being near her and they love working with her. Thanks to Mrs. Cottontail and Nurse Feelwell, Penelope Proctor is one of the happiest and most popular little bunnies at Stephen B. O'Hare Elementary School.

DISCUSSION QUESTIONS

1. What kind of problem did Penelope have? *(She did not take care of her body or her surroundings.)*

2. Why didn't her parents help her with her problem? *(They had the same problem.)*

3. How were the animals at Penelope's new school different from the ones at her old school? *(They did not call her mean names or tease her.)*

4. Why didn't anyone tell Penelope there was food in her teeth? *(They thought it would be impolite.)*

5. Who was Jimmy Jumper and what did he do? *(Jimmy Jumper was a classmate who fell on the floor laughing when he saw the food between Penelope's teeth.)*

6. Why wouldn't the girls trade lunches with Penelope? *(She did not wash her paws before eating and they thought her food might not be clean.)*

7. Why did Reyna ask to talk with Mrs. Cottontail? *(She told Mrs. Cottontail that Penelope did not smell very fresh.)*

8. What was the Proctor home like? *(There were dirty dishes, food on the floors and walls, grease on the stove, and the whole house was untidy.)*

9. Was Mrs. Proctor kind? *(Yes.)* Did she have good manners? *(No.)*

10. How did Mrs. Cottontail and Mrs. Feelwell help the Proctor family? *(They invited them to a health fair at the school, where they learned good health habits.)*

FOLLOW-UP ACTIVITIES

1. **Penelope Proctor's Problem:** Reproduce *Penelope Proctor's Problem Matching Activity* (page 35) for each student. Distribute a copy of the activity sheet and a pencil to each student. Have the students draw a line from the word on the left to the correct answer on the right. The answers are: Floss-d; Soap-b; Toothpaste-none; Toothbrush-c; Mouthwash-g; Shampoo-f; Perfume-e; Cologne-a; Washcloth-j; Brush-h; Comb-i.

2. **Cause And Effect:** The following questions are written to stimulate the students' thinking in terms of themselves and their own personal hygiene. Use them as a class-discussion activity.

    1. What would happen if you used only a toothbrush and no toothpaste to clean your teeth? *(Your teeth would not get clean.)*

    2. What would happen if you used shampoo without water to wash your hair? *(You could not rinse the shampoo from your hair and your hair would remain dirty.)*

    3. Should you use mouthwash to wash your hands? *(No. Mouthwash will not get your hands clean.)*

    4. Can you use a comb to clean your teeth? *(No, it could hurt the enamel on your teeth and your teeth will not get clean.)*

    5. Should you bathe with dental floss? *(No, it will not get your body clean.)*

    6. What would happen if you forgot to put on deodorant? *(Adults who perspire and do not use deodorant may have body odor.)*

    7. If you bathed without soap, would you be clean? *(No.)*

    8. What could happen if you never washed your hands before eating lunch? *(You could get germs on your food, and you could get sick.)*

    9. What happens if you put on too much perfume or cologne? *(You have too strong a smell.)*

    10. What could happen if you ate from dirty dishes? *(You could get germs that could make you sick.)*

PENELOPE PROCTOR'S PROBLEM
MATCHING ACTIVITY

Directions: Draw a line from the word on the left to the correct answer on the right. One of the words on the left does not have an answer on the right.

Floss

Toothpaste

Toothbrush

Mouthwash

Shampoo

Soap

Perfume

Cologne

Washcloth

Brush

Comb

a. a scented fragrance for boys

b. lathers up and helps clean the germs from your body

c. tool used with paste to polish and clean teeth

d. used to clean between teeth

e. used by girls to help them smell pretty

f. used to clean hair

g. liquid used to freshen breath

h. a tool with bristles used to smooth hair

i. a tool with teeth used to detangle hair

j. textured cloth used to scrub your body clean

THE I CAN'T
GRADES 2-3

RESPONSIBILITY

WRITTEN BY DENA M. HALL

Dena M. Hall is a freelance writer whose daughter's teacher encouraged her to submit this poem for publication. Her poems have also been published by The Iowa Chapter of the National Committee to Prevent Child Abuse, The Foster Family Forum, and Feature Films For Families. She is the mother of four children and resides in Iowa.

THE I CAN'T

A long time ago
There was a little lad
Who didn't do much
Without help from Mom and Dad.

When he tried to do something
And couldn't get it right,
He would get mad and yell
"I can't!" with all his might.

Now Mom and Dad loved him
And wanted him not to act that way.
So they did everything for him.
Every single day.

One day, he woke up
And didn't hear a sound
He walked through the house.
No one was around!

Oh, me! Oh, my!
What will I do?
Who will get me dressed?
Who will tie my shoes?

He tried to get dressed,
But he couldn't do it right.
So he yelled over and over,
"I can't!" with all his might.

Then out of nowhere it appeared!
Down from the ceiling it came.
It was a fuzzy little man.
THE I CAN'T was his name.

"Hello, J. J.," he said,
Landing right on the boy's knee,
"I came because I heard
You calling for me!"

"Who are you?" asked J. J.
With great surprise.
"You came out of nowhere
Right before my eyes."

"I'm THE I CAN'T!
Don't you see?
Nothing ever gets done
If you act like me."

"Come with me
And I'll show you the way
To do absolutely nothing
every single day!"

So away with THE I CAN'T
J. J. then flew.
He liked the idea
Of having nothing to do.

At first J. J. liked
Living this way,
Sitting around
In his pajamas all day.

At first he thought
Being lazy was neat.
But then he got hungry
And wanted something to eat.

"Will you dress me and feed me
As fast as you can?"
J. J. called out
To the fuzzy little man.

"I want to go out
And see the town.
But I can't do it
In my nightgown."

THE I CAN'T appeared
As fast as before.
"I can't" he told J. J.,
And said nothing more.

J. J. was afraid
And he started to cry.
Then THE I CAN'T smiled
And asked, "Why don't *you* try?"

J. J. didn't know
What he should do.
Trying to do something himself
Was very new.

So he picked out some clothes
And he got out his shoes.
"Here goes," he thought,
"I've got nothing to lose!"

He took a deep breath
And tried with all his might.
This time it happened.
He did it all right!

His face shone, and his eyes did, too.
He felt so great! He felt so good!
He said, "I can't" no more,
Because he knew that he could!

DISCUSSION QUESTIONS

1. What are some things you can do all by yourself? *(Accept any appropriate answers.)*

2. What is something you need help to do? *(Accept any appropriate answers.)*

3. When should you ask for help? *(You should ask for help when you are absolutely sure you cannot do something or when it is something your parents have told you not to do without their help.)*

4. Who is someone you can ask for help? *(Accept any appropriate answers.)*

5. When should you do something for yourself? *(You should do anything that you are capable of doing for yourself.)*

6. Instead of saying "I can't," what could you say? *(I can.)*

7. What is it called when you do things for yourself? *(It is called accepting responsibility.)*

FOLLOW-UP ACTIVITIES

1. **The I Can Can:** Decorate a coffee can. Have each of the students write something they can do by themselves on a slip of paper. If the students cannot write, have them draw a picture of what they can do. Place the slips of paper in the can. Pull out one slip of paper at a time and tell the students what is written/drawn on it. To make the activity more interesting, do not tell the students the name of the person who wrote/drew on the slip of paper. Instead, have the students guess whose paper each slip is. Each time an act is explained, say, "(STUDENT'S NAME) has shown us that by (IDENTIFY ACT), he/she is responsible."

2. **Yes, You Can:** Tell the students to think of something they can do by themselves. (For example: brush hair, fix a drink, tie a shoe.) Choose a student and instruct him/her to say: "Can I (NAME OF SOMETHING THE STUDENT CAN DO BY HIM/HERSELF)?" The leader replies, "Yes, you can!" The student then acts out or does the thing he/she has been told he/she can do. Each time an act is explained/acted out, the leader says, "(STUDENT'S NAME) has shown us that by (IDENTIFY ACT), he/she is responsible."

I CAN DECIDE ... IT'S UP TO ME
GRADES 3-5

DECISION-MAKING
RESPONSIBILITY

WRITTEN BY WANDA S. COOK

Wanda Cook is an elementary counselor in Texas. She is a contributor to *Special Situations*, published by Mar*co Products.

 MAR*CO PRODUCTS, INC. © 2002 1-800-448-2197

I CAN DECIDE ... IT'S UP TO ME

I can decide about many things.
I can make choices.

I can decide to wear my blue cap with the big white star or my white cap with the big blue star.

I can decide to snack on a sweet, delicious apple or a handful of crunchy nuts.

I can decide to watch a very funny movie or one that's just a little bit spooky.

I can decide to play football with Frank or baseball with Brittany.

What I decide is up to me.

These are easy choices.

But some choices are *not* so easy ... especially the ones I make at school.

This morning, I had to decide if I should think about my spelling work or think about my new silver scooter.

Then, later, I had to decide if I should listen to Peter's jokes or listen to Mrs. Smith explain our math projects.

During lunch, I had to decide if I should keep the dollar bill I found on the table or turn it in to the Lost and Found.

And after science class, I had to decide if I should close the door on the hamster's cage or let it chase Margaret around the room.

Some choices are harder than others.

But I can decide!

It's all up to me.

Before I decide, I think about what will happen after I make each choice.

I think about how my choices will make others feel.

I think about those who believe in me.

Then I decide what to do.

I decided to finish my spelling work and think about my scooter later.

I decided to listen to Mrs. Smith instead of to Peter.

I decided to turn in the dollar bill so that others will trust me.

And I decided to close the door on the hamster's cage so that Margaret wouldn't be afraid.

When I choose to do the right thing, I feel good about my choices.

But sometimes I don't feel so good about my choices.

Like at home, when Mom tells me to clean my room and I stuff my junk underneath my bed instead.

Or when I decide to play videogames instead of taking out the kitchen trash.

And one time when I got mad at my little brother, I hid his glasses underneath the sofa cushion.

Sometimes I don't stop and think about what will happen after I make a choice.

Sometimes I don't stop and think about how my choices will make others feel.

Sometimes I only think about me.

When I decided not to clean my room, Mom decided that I couldn't go fishing with Uncle Buzz.

When I decided not to take out the trash, the bags leaked and the kitchen got all messy.

And when I decided to hide my little brother's glasses, Aunt Gertrude accidentally sat on them.

There are consequences of making bad choices.

So I learn from my mistakes. And the next time, I make better choices.

And Mom, my little brother, and Aunt Gertrude understand.

As I grow older, my choices will be even harder to make.

Mom says that others may ask me to try things that are bad for my body or ask me to do things that are silly or unsafe.

But she says that I can still make the right choices.

As long as I remember to ...

Think about what will happen after I make each choice.

Think about how my choices will make others feel.

Think about those who believe in me.

And think about me!

Sometimes I will make mistakes. But I will learn from my mistakes and make better choices the next time.

That's all part of growing up, you know.

Dad says that one day I'll make other important choices like where to work, where to live, and who should run our country.

Aunt Gertrude says that one day I'll even have to decide whom I am going to marry.

I said, "YUK!"

Each day, I'm learning how important it is to make good choices at home, at school, or when I'm hanging out with my friends.

And I am learning how important my choices will be when I'm older.

Whether my choices are easy choices, hard choices, or future choices, they are important choices.

And before I choose:

 MAR*CO PRODUCTS, INC. © 2002 1-800-448-2197

I will think about what will happen after I make each choice.

I will think about how my choices will make others feel.

I will think about those who believe in me.

And I will think about me!

I will choose to do the right thing.

I will make good choices.

I can decide.

It's all up to me!

DISCUSSION QUESTIONS

1. What three choices did you make at home this morning? *(Accept any appropriate answers.)*

2. Which choice was the hardest to make? Why? *(Accept any appropriate answers.)*

3. What three choices have you made at school today? *(Accept any appropriate answers.)*

4. Which choice was the hardest to make? Why? *(Accept any appropriate answers.)*

5. Which choice have you made that made you proud of yourself? *(Accept any appropriate answers.)*

6. Which choice have you made that did not make you proud of yourself? *(Accept any appropriate answers.)*

7. What happens when you make bad choices? *(When you make bad choices, you get in trouble, people get hurt or are sad, you feel bad.)*

8. What should you do before you make a difficult choice? *(Think about what will happen after you make the choice, how the choice will make others feel, how it will make you feel.)*

9. Are all choices easy to make? Why or why not? *(Accept any appropriate answers.)*

10. If someone offers you drugs or other things that are harmful to your body, what choice would you make? *(Accept any appropriate answers.)*

11. What could happen if you make the wrong choice? *(Accept any appropriate answers.)*

12. What are some important choices you will make in the future? *(Accept any appropriate answers.)*

FOLLOW-UP ACTIVITY

1. **If You Decide ...:** Read the following sentences aloud. Tell the students to think about how each choice will affect others. Discuss each situation.

   1. If you decide to cause trouble in school ...

   2. If you decide not to turn in a homework assignment ...

   3. If you decide not to study for your spelling test and to cheat from your neighbor's paper ...

   4. If you decide to take Sally's ham sandwich from her lunchbox and eat it instead of eating the tuna sandwich in your own lunchbox ...

   5. If you decide not to share the ball during recess ...

   6. If you decide to tear up your math paper because you are angry ...

   7. If you decide not to tie your shoe laces because it's not the cool thing to do ...

   8. If you decide not to shower and change your clothes ...

   9. If you decide to wait until the last minute to complete an important assignment ...

   10. If you decide to watch cartoons all night and not get enough sleep ...

BLAME IT ON BLAKE
GRADES 3-5

HONESTY
RESPONSIBILITY

WRITTEN BY SHIRLEY REDCAY

Shirley Redcay is an elementary counselor in Florida. She is the author of *Friendship Fables* and a contributing author to *Special Situations*, both published by Mar∗co Products.

BLAME IT ON BLAKE

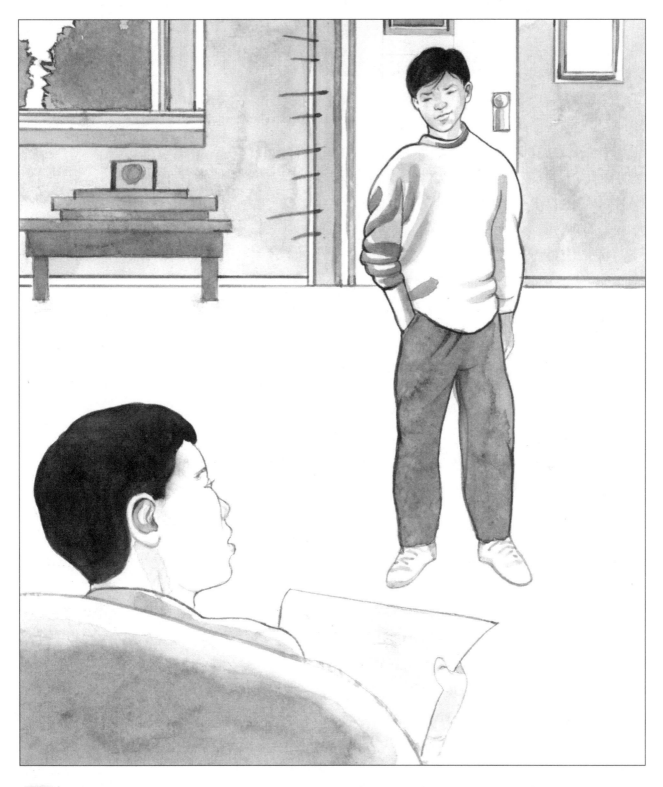

Blake had hardly opened the door before he heard his dad ask, "How was your day, Blake?"

"It happened again today, Dad," Blake complained, throwing his backpack on the table with a smack. "Someone let the gerbil out of its cage. And when the teacher asked who did it, everyone said, 'Blake did it'."

"Did you do it?" Dad asked calmly.

"No! I mean, it was an accident. I didn't mean to do it. I just moved the cage a little, and I must have bumped the latch. But I didn't really let it out," Blake defended himself.

"What did you tell the teacher?" asked Dad.

"I just said I didn't do it. She never believes me, anyway. But I'm going to get everyone back tomorrow. It's my turn to be class monitor. I'll figure out something bad I can write about each one of them. I'm going to get everyone else in trouble so they'll know how it feels," Blake threatened.

"Whoa, Blake!" Dad cautioned. "Will that really make things better for you?"

"No. Nobody can make things better for me, but at least I can make things worse for the rest of them," moaned Blake.

"Blake, it sounds like you're too angry to think right now. Let's go shoot some hoops to calm down," suggested Dad. "Then we'll talk about tomorrow."

"OK, but only if you order pizza for dinner," Blake bargained, as he began spinning the basketball on his finger.

"It's a deal," agreed Dad. "Pizza sounds good to me, too. I'll order it now, then it will be here by the time we've worked up an appetite playing ball."

Just as the two of them were ready to collapse, the pizza delivery truck came into view. Dad paid for the pizza and carried it to the kitchen counter. "Blake, put the ball away. You know the rules. No tossing it in the house," warned Dad.

As Dad opened the pizza box, Blake gave one last toss of the ball. It slipped out of his hands and landed right in the middle of the pizza.

"Blake ...," Dad started to say, before Blake interrupted him.

"It wasn't my fault, Dad. It slipped. I couldn't help it," Blake tried to explain. "It was an accident."

"Blake, following directions would have prevented that *accident*," Dad started to say when Blake interrupted him again.

"Oh, no! Here comes the lecture," moaned Blake.

"Blake, I'm not sure you would listen if I *did* lecture. Why don't you give the lecture and I'll listen?" Dad suggested.

"Do you really mean it?" a shocked Blake asked.

"Sure. Use your common sense. What would you tell me if I had tossed the ball that ruined our dinner?" asked Dad.

"Can I ground you forever?" kidded Blake.

"Is that what you think I should do?" asked Dad.

"No way! But if I were the dad, I'd make you clean up the mess and pay for another pizza out of my own allowance ... I mean *your* allowance," laughed Blake.

"Blake, that is a very responsible solution," said Dad. "But there is one more thing to do."

"What's that?" asked Blake.

"Take responsibility for your own actions. Don't blame the ball," Dad directed.

"I'm sorry, Dad," apologized Blake. "I shouldn't have been playing with the ball in the house."

"Apology accepted," said Dad. "Now was that so hard?"

"No, but you don't tease me like the kids do at school," answered Blake.

"Do you believe you've earned their respect?" asked Dad. "I think if you take more responsibility for your actions at school, you will gain their respect and the teacher's, too. Then they will be more likely to believe you and you won't have to worry so much about getting blamed for things you didn't do."

"But it seems like I'm always getting in trouble. My teacher says I don't listen," Blake complained.

"Do you think that might be your ticket out of trouble?" suggested Dad.

"You mean *listening*? I hear what she says," Blake answered.

"Hearing what someone says in an important start. But a good listener makes use of the information that's been heard," continued Dad. "You heard me say not to toss the ball in the house, but you did not use the information. You did not do what I asked."

"I know, but I thought one more time wouldn't hurt," Blake said, trying to justify his actions.

"Do you remember *Simon Says*, the game we used to play when you were little?" asked Dad.

"Sure," replied Blake. "I was really good at it."

"Well, you play it in school every day, just in a different way," explained Dad.

"I get it! I get it!" Blake said excitedly. "The teacher is Simon, and I have to follow her directions."

"That's right. And if you mess up, be honest and admit it," Dad added.

"I made a real mess out of that pizza," Blake admitted as he lifted his basketball off the cheese. "I'll clean this up. Will you order another one?"

"I will. But guess who is paying for it?" Dad reminded him.

"I know," agreed Blake. "And while I'm waiting for the pizza, I think I will write an apology to my teacher about what happened to the gerbil. And I'll tell her I'll be the most honest class monitor she ever had. Even if I have to report myself."

DISCUSSION QUESTIONS

1. How did Blake cause his own problems? *(He did not follow instructions and did not take responsibility for his own actions.)*

2. What could have happened if he had used his idea for taking revenge on his classmates? *(Accept any appropriate answers.)*

3. What positive character traits are mentioned in the story? *(The story refers to respect, responsibility, and honesty.)*

4. What are some other positive character traits? *(Accept any appropriate answers.)*

5. What character quality would you like to develop more in your own life? *(Accept any appropriate answers.)*

FOLLOW-UP ACTIVITIES

1. **Write About It:** Distribute paper and pencils to the students and ask each of them to write what they believe happened to Blake the next day at school.

2. **Story Skit:** Reproduce two copies of the story. Highlight Blake's dialogue on one copy and Dad's dialogue on the other. Select two students to act out the parts as they read their copies. For more realism, use a pizza box and a basketball as props.

3. **Simon Says:** Play a game of *Simon Says.* See who can best follow directions.

4. **Listening:** Play a game of *Listening.* Distribute paper and pencils to the students and ask them to be very quiet. Then tell them to write down all the sounds they can hear around them in the next five minutes. Try this game, if possible, both indoors and outdoors.

MY FEEL-GOOD BOOK
GRADES 1-3

SELF-RESPECT

WRITTEN BY SHEILA HEALY

Sheila Healy is a certified social worker in New York.

Note: This lesson requires some pre-presentation preparation. Before beginning the lesson, compile booklets of 10 blank pages and the two activity pages (pages 66-67) for each student. Distribute a booklet, crayons, and a pencil to each student. On the first page of the booklet, have the students write: "MY FEEL-GOOD BOOK by _____" and add their name. Then proceed with the story.

MY FEEL-GOOD BOOK

Sally feels sad and yucky today. She thinks no one likes her and she feels that she is not a good person.

She is very sad and feels all alone. There are a lot of people like Sally who do not feel good about themselves. People who don't feel good about themselves, like Sally, do not have a strong or positive *self-esteem*. The way we look at ourselves is called our self-esteem. Sometimes people do not feel good about themselves. They may feel sad, lonely, or angry. They may think things about themselves like, "I am no good." "I am not pretty or cute." "No one likes me."

On the next page of your booklet, draw a picture about a time when you did not feel good about yourself. At the top of your picture, write, "How I Look When I Don't Feel Good About Myself."

Sometimes people "put themselves down" or say negative things about themselves. They might say, "I am no good," or "I am a terrible ball player." Words like this can make you feel bad about yourself. Do you "put yourself down"?

Pause in order for the students to think silently about an answer to the question.

When we start to think yucky things about ourselves, we can tell ourselves to STOP! and try to think good things about ourselves. Practice doing this when you are feeling yucky.

Sally puts herself down a lot and thinks bad things about herself. This makes Sally feel even sadder and more yucky!

Sometimes when Sally is thinking negative things about herself, she tells herself to STOP and tries to think good thoughts. This helps Sally feel better. Sally really wants to be happy and feel good about herself. She is trying hard not to think yucky things about herself.

Sally thinks good things about herself to make herself feel happy. When she is having a bad day, she says something positive in her head, over and over again, until she feels better. This is called *self-talk*. The messages we send to ourselves or think in our heads are called *self-talk*.

It can help us feel better about ourselves if we say positive things to ourselves. Having a lot of negative self-talk can make us feel yucky about ourselves. Saying a lot of good things about ourselves can help us feel good.

Tell the students to think of one good thing about themselves. Tell them to say this good thing out loud three times when you give a signal.

Sally is trying to do something nice for herself every day. When Sally does something nice for herself, she reminds herself that she is special. Every day, Sally listens to music and relaxes in her room. This makes her feel good.

Many things can make us feel good. You might feel good when you exercise, take a relaxing bath, get dressed up for a special occasion, or get your hair cut.

Draw a picture that shows you doing one thing for yourself that makes you feel good. At the top of your picture, write, "This Makes Me Feel Good About Me."

Sally has some friends who make her feel yucky by calling her names. Sally tries not to let their words hurt her feelings. She tells herself that she is a wonderful person and tries to stay away from people who hurt her feelings.

Sally also has people in her life who make her feel very happy. She has a very nice friend named Timmy. Timmy always has a nice smile for Sally. He is a good friend to her. He is kind to Sally, says nice things to her, and listens to her when she is having a problem. Sally likes to be around Timmy because he makes her feel good.

Sometimes there are people in our lives who tell us yucky things and do not make us feel good. Maybe there is someone in your life who says yucky or mean things to you. How does that person's words make you feel?

Pause for answers to the question. Then tell the students to draw a picture showing a time someone said something yucky or mean to them, and, at the top of the picture, write the words, "A Time Someone Said Something Yucky To Me."

Sometimes there are people in our lives who help us feel good about ourselves by offering their love, support, and encouragement. Can you think of a family member or a friend who is there for you during tough times? Does this person make you feel good about yourself?

Tell the students to draw a picture about a time this "special person" made them feel good about themselves. At the top of their paper, they should write the words, "(NAME OF THE SPECIAL PERSON) Makes Me Feel Good."

Sally feels good when someone says something nice to her or gives her a compliment. The other day, a friend told Sally that she looked very pretty in her red dress. These words made Sally feel wonderful! When she is having a bad day, Sally tries to remember compliments people have given her.

It feels good when people say nice things about each other or give each other compliments. For example, someone might tell you that you look nice today or that you are a nice person.

Tell the students to think about a time someone said something nice about them, then draw a picture about this time. At the top of their paper, they should write the words, "A Time Someone Said Something Nice To Me."

Sally likes to make other people feel good. Every day, she tries to do something nice for someone or say something nice to someone. The other day, she told her friend Timmy that he was the greatest friend in the world. This made both Sally and Timmy feel good.

Saying nice things to other people can help us feel good. You might try to say something nice to someone every day. If you could say something nice to someone today, what would you say and to whom would you say it?

Tell the students to draw a picture of the person to whom they would say something nice, then write the name of the person and what they would say above the drawing.

Sally used to do anything to get attention, even if it was negative attention. Sally used to throw temper tantrums or goof around when she was not supposed to. She knew if she did those things, she could get attention.

Sally stopped doing yucky things to get attention because she realized that she could get attention by doing positive things instead. Now Sally gets attention by being kind to others or doing good deeds. Sally baked a yummy pie for her friends and got some positive attention for doing it.

Good friendships are one thing that can help make people feel connected and important.

_____

Tell the students to write three things that they think other people like or admire about them.

_____

People often need attention to make them feel good, loved, and happy. Sometimes people will even do yucky or negative things to get attention. Do you ever act yucky or do negative things to attract attention?

_____

Tell the students to draw a picture of a time they wanted attention and acted yucky to get someone to notice them.

_____

Sometimes it is hard to get positive attention from people. People want attention to feel good and loved. There are a lot of good and positive ways to get people to notice you. What are some good ways to get people to notice you and give you attention?

_____

Tell the students to write down some good ways to get people to notice them.

_____

We are all special. Sally is learning about why she is special. Sally has thought of a bunch of reasons why she is special. Some of these reasons are: I am a good person; I am funny; I am pretty; I am smart; I am nice; and I am a good friend.

Sally has learned a lot about having self-esteem and feeling good. She tries not to say bad things about herself. If she does say bad things about herself, she tells herself to STOP!

When Sally is feeling yucky, she tries to think of good things about herself. Sally realizes that she is normal and is not perfect. She knows it is okay to make mistakes. Sally tries to get attention from people she loves in positive ways. She is happy with herself and feels much, much, much better. Do *you* feel better?

Sally now believes that she is a great person. She knows that she can make friends because she is nice, fun, and cares about others.

Tell the students to complete their booklets by completing the sentences on the last two pages of their booklets. When all the students have finished, have some of them share their answers with the group. At the end of the period, allow the students to take their booklets home.

What I Have Learned From This Book

By _____

I am special because _____

_____

_____ .

Other people like me because _____

_____

_____ .

If I start to think yucky things about myself, I can tell

myself this four-letter word: _____ .

If I start to feel yucky about myself, I can change my thinking and say something good about myself like

_____

_____

_____ .

One thing I can do for myself to make me feel good is

_____

_____ .

If I need support or need to hear good things, I can turn to _____

_____ .

I know how to get positive attention when I need it. If I need attention, I can_____

_____

_____ .

Every day, I will try to think positive thoughts like

_____

_____

_____ .

JEREMIAH CAN'T FLY
GRADES 2-4

SEPARATION ANXIETY
SELF-CONFIDENCE

WRITTEN BY LISA BALL

Lisa Ball is a counselor in Georgia.

JEREMIAH CAN'T FLY

Once there was a bird family: a mother and her three beautiful babies—Jake, Jenny, and Jeremiah.

Mother Bird would leave the nest every morning in search of food. She told her babies to stay in the nest, because it was very dangerous outside. The baby birds were very frightened while their mother was gone. However, she came home every day with worms and hugs for them all.

As the baby birds grew, the time came for them to step out of the nest. The small birds were very frightened, because they were not sure what would happen to them. Mother Bird went first to Jake. She nudged him gently. Finally, Jake took a deep breath, left the nest, and made his way onto a branch.

Seeing Jake, Jenny felt sure that she could do the same thing. So without a second thought, she hopped out onto the wobbly branch. Her knees were shaky. With one more step, she slipped and fell to the ground. Her mother, Jake, and other forest friends hurried to her side. Jenny was fine. She dusted herself off and jumped right back onto the wobbly branch. She knew that she could do it, and that if she fell, others would help her.

Jeremiah was still in the nest. "Please, Mother, don't make me go," he pleaded. "I don't think I can." Mother hugged Jeremiah and said, "It's all right, Jeremiah. You don't have to try to fly today."

During the next several days, Jake and Jenny got used to going out. They began to fly, and soon were playing with other little birds. But not Jeremiah. He was still too afraid to come out. He wanted to join the others. But as soon as he put one foot over the nest, his stomach began hurting. Mother Bird tried very hard to encourage him, but he only felt safe when he stayed in the nest.

Jeremiah continued to grow. He was getting bigger and bigger. Mother Bird was staying away from the nest more and more because Jeremiah was eating more and more and she had to work harder to feed him. Meanwhile, Jeremiah was becoming lonely. He could see the other birds from his nest, but he was too afraid to join them. Jake and Jenny were learning many new things that helped them stay safe when they were away from the nest. Jeremiah was only learning new excuses for staying home.

Soon Jeremiah was too big for his mother's nest. Other birds would fly by and make fun of how his body overflowed the little nest. Jeremiah was miserable. Suddenly he realized that staying at home never made the outside less scary. He knew that only by getting out and learning skills that would help him deal with the world would he gain a sense of safety. So he decided to fly.

Slowly, he pulled one leg over the edge of the nest. Then the other leg followed. It felt like a strange thing, but Jeremiah was doing it. He had a lump in his throat. He flapped his wings and began to whistle. "Look, everyone!" he yelled. "I'm doing it!"

Suddenly, the branch cracked. Jeremiah lost his balance. And as he could not hold on any longer, he fell to the ground. When Jeremiah looked up from the ground, he saw that several birds had come to help him get back on his feet. Even if he wasn't a great success, just making the effort made Jeremiah feel very proud of himself.

As the days passed, it became easier and easier for Jeremiah to get out of the nest. At times, he felt like asking his mother to let him stay home. But then he remembered that every day that he didn't leave the nest was a day that he might miss learning a new skill that would make his life better.

DISCUSSION QUESTIONS

1. When did it become clear that Jeremiah was different from his brother and sister? *(It became clear when it was time for them to leave the nest. Jeremiah was too frightened to try to fly.)*

2. How was Jeremiah different from Jake and Jenny? *(He did not have confidence in himself.)*

3. What is *self-confidence*? *(Self-confidence is believing in yourself and in your ability to do new things.)*

4. What finally made Jeremiah leave the nest? *(He was lonely, the other birds made fun of him, and he grew too big to stay in the nest.)*

5. Was Jeremiah successful the first time he left the nest? *(No. He fell to the ground.)*

6. What made him keep trying? *(He knew others would help him if he needed help.)*

7. By staying in the nest, Jeremiah not only didn't learn to fly, he did not learn how to take care of himself. What skills, other than flying, do you think birds need to know? *(They need to know how to find food, protect themselves from dangers, build a nest, etc.)*

8. What is your nest? *(Your home is your nest.)*

9. If you did not want to leave your home, what would you never learn? *(Accept any appropriate answers about school, safety, social skills, etc.)*

FOLLOW-UP ACTIVITIES

1. **Self-Confidence And Lack Of Self-Confidence:** Divide the students into groups. Have each group elect a spokesperson. Distribute paper and a pencil to that person. Remind the groups that having self-confidence is believing in yourself and in your ability to accomplish new tasks. Ask each group to think of as many feeling words as possible in three minutes to describe a person who is not self-confident. Tell each spokesperson to write down the group's contributions. At the end of that time, tell the spokesperson to turn the paper over and write down, in three minutes, all of the feeling words mentioned by the group that describe a self-confident person. When everyone has finished, ask each group to complete the following sentence stem:

    It is better to be self-confident than not self-confident because _____ .

    When each group has completed the sentence stem, have each spokesperson read its group's completed sentence.

2. **Self-Confidence Would Help Me Learn To:** Reproduce *Self-Confidence Would Help Me Learn To ...*(page 75) for each student. Distribute a copy of the activity sheet, a pencil, and crayons to each student. Tell the students to think of one thing that they do not do right now, but would like to do in the future. Have them draw a picture of what that thing is, then answer the questions at the bottom of the page.

Name _____

SELF-CONFIDENCE WOULD HELP ME LEARN TO ...

Here is a picture of something I would like to do in the future:

[ ]

I would like to be able to do this when I am _____ years old.

Two things I will need to learn in order to do this are:

_____

_____

These two things will help me have the self-confidence I will need to meet my future goal.

MISS PRISS AND THE COPYCATS
GRADES 1-3

INDEPENDENCE
PEER PRESSURE
DECISION-MAKING

WRITTEN BY PATRICIA PETTY

Patricia Petty is a counselor in a K-3 primary school in Tennessee. She writes her stories when preparing classroom-guidance lessons.

MISS PRISS AND THE COPYCATS

Miss Priss was happy with her new class. The school year was just beginning and all the kittens looked happy and ready to learn.

They found friends quickly and had lots of fun together in the schoolyard. The kittens tossed balls around and played games of tag. They knew that exercise was not only fun, but also made them feel good.

As the days passed, it was easy to see that each kitten was different and special in its own way. Miss Priss spent time learning to know each one of her students by the way they looked, spoke, and acted. Each day seemed happier than the day before.

One day, Miss Priss was *not* happy. Her class had a day full of problems. The kittens had Center Time, when they went to tables and worked on special projects. But today, when Center Time was over, the classroom looked like a giant spider web. It was covered with yarn!

"Oh my!" said Miss Priss. "What happened here?" Gary Gray spoke up, "Well, the group at Center One threw the balls of yarn to us at Center Two. They were laughing really hard. We got covered with yarn. They told us to throw the balls on to Center Three. They were laughing so much, we thought it must be fun. So we threw the balls and covered some more kittens with yarn."

Miss Priss, who wasn't laughing, asked, "Will it be fun to clean up this mess? This is supposed to be your play time, but now that is all changed. Now it is cleanup time."

Tina Tabby, from Center Three, said, "It would be more fun to play."

Gary Gray said, "I wish we had told the kittens from Center One, NO! Thinking about it now, it really *wasn't* fun to be tangled up in yarn."

As if the yarn incident weren't enough, Miss Priss heard a report from the lunchroom after lunch. The report said that her class had been howling in the lunchroom. When she asked the class what happened, Tommy Tiger answered, "We only howled after Mr. Ruff's class howled. After all, the pups dared us to try to howl louder than they did."

Miss Priss thought silently for a few moments. Then she said, "Hmmm, hmmmm, I think I know what's happened. My kittens are turning into copycats—and they are copying the wrong things! What do *you* think?"

Gary, Tina, Tommy, and the other kittens agreed that they had been copying the wrong behaviors. Gary spoke first, "I wish we had said NO to the kittens at Center One. I just *knew* it would be a bad idea to throw yarn around the room." Then Tommy spoke. "I wish we had said NO to the pups in the lunchroom," he said. "I knew that howling would get us in trouble." Finally, Tina spoke, "I don't want to be a copycat. My mama and papa have always told me to think for myself. They say that is being *independent*. It means doing my own thing, especially when I know the right thing to do." Miss Priss knew Tina Tabby was right. So did all of the other kittens.

Miss Priss thought to herself, "Maybe today was not such a bad day. The things my kittens did today taught them a very important lesson. Now I know they will grow to be fine cats. I'm glad the bad day helped them learn that being a copycat does not always mean being a *happy* cat!"

DISCUSSION QUESTIONS

1. What are the things Miss Priss noticed that made each of her students different? *(They looked, spoke, and acted differently.)* Would this be true for the students in your class? *(Yes.)*

2. How did Miss Priss' classroom get to be a mess? *(The kittens threw balls of yarn around the room.)*

3. What did Miss Priss do about the mess? *(She made the kittens take responsibility for their behavior and clean up the mess instead of having play time.)*

4. What did Tina Tabby think about the mess? *(Tina thought it would have been more fun to play than to clean up the mess.)*

5. What was the problem reported to Miss Priss from the lunchroom? *(The kittens had been howling.)*

6. Why were the kittens howling in the lunchroom? *(They were howling because Mr. Ruff's class had dared them to try to howl louder than they were howling.)*

7. What did the kittens think about the howling? *(They thought they should not have done it.)*

8. Tina said she learned that cats should be independent. What does being independent mean? *(It means thinking for yourself and not doing what others want, if what they are asking you to do is wrong.)*

9. What lesson did Miss Priss' kittens learn from their bad day? *(They learned not to be copycats when what they were copying was wrong.)*

FOLLOW-UP ACTIVITIES

1. **Copy Cat Art Activity:** Play a game of *Copycat* with the students. Distribute art paper and crayons to each student. Tell the students that you are going to give them some directions. They are to be copycats and do exactly what you say. Then proceed with the following 10 directions:

    1. Write your name in blue crayon at the top of your paper.
    2. Draw a green triangle on your paper.
    3. Cross out three letters of your name.
    4. Write the numbers from *1* to *5* in black crayon.
    5. Write the numbers from *5* to *1* in yellow crayon.
    6. Drop your paper on the floor and step on it hard.
    7. Pick up your paper and crumple it.
    8. Straighten your paper and draw three red circles.
    9. Put four dots in each circle, using any crayon you wish.
    10. Tear your paper into four pieces.

    Go back over the directions one at a time, asking the students if each one is a direction they should copy. The numbers of the directions not to be copied are 3, 6, 7, and 10. Have the students explain why following these directions ruins the paper on which they are working. Conclude the activity by telling the students it is good to be a copycat only if what they are copying is something good.

2. **Copycat:** Reproduce *I Won't Be A Copycat ...* (page 83) for each student. Distribute a copy of the activity sheet, a pencil, and crayons to each student. Have the students complete the activity sheet either by drawing pictures or writing words. When everyone has finished the activity, have them share their work with the group.

I WON'T BE A COPYCAT ...

When I see others making the wrong choices in class, like these:

Or in the lunchroom, like these:

I WILL BE INDEPENDENT ...

And make the right choices in class, like these:

And in the lunchroom, like these:

THE ADVENTURES OF ELSIE THE ELEPHANT AND HER TROUBLESOME TRUNK

GRADES 1-3

TOLERANCE
CARING
SELF-CONFIDENCE

WRITTEN BY JENNIFER L. MOTT

Jennifer Mott is an elementary counselor in Wisconsin. She frequently writes her own stories for both individual and group-counseling sessions.

THE ADVENTURES OF ELSIE THE ELEPHANT AND HER TROUBLESOME TRUNK

Elsie the elephant and Zol the zebra walked down the path through the grasslands one bright sunny day. These two best friends were looking forward to a day of fun on their day off from school. As they talked about their plans for the day, they noticed a group of lions coming their way.

As Elsie and Zol got closer to the lions, one lion shouted, "Look at the freak with the mile-long trunk and huge ears! I've never seen an animal look so ridiculous in my whole life! What happened to your face?" As the other lions laughed and pointed at Elsie, she stared at the ground and started to cry.

As her face turned bright red and tears ran down her cheeks, Elsie ran away from the group. She'd never felt so embarrassed in her whole life. Stopping by the edge of the pond, she looked at her reflection. Zol followed and sat down beside her. "I'm sorry that those lions were so mean. I wish I could have done something, but I was scared they would start teasing me, too," said Zol.

"It's OK. I just keep thinking about how silly I look with my huge trunk and ears," sniffed Elsie. "Those lions were right. I *am* the most ridiculous-looking animal. Why can't I look normal, like you?"

Zol gave her friend a caring look. "Elsie, I love your beautiful floppy ears. You are SO lucky! You can cool yourself off whenever you want. And what a trunk! Your trunk can pick up anything!" Looking sad, Zol said, "If you want to know the truth, I've always wished I were only one color, instead of this black-and-white pattern. Everyone gawks at me! Sometimes I think I should join the circus. Then people would have to pay money to stare and point at me!"

Jon the giraffe met up with Elsie and Zol and yelled, "Hey, why all the sad faces? It's a beautiful day, and there's no school!"

Zol responded, "Hi, Jon. We know we should feel happy about today, but it's kind of hard to feel excited about our day off when the lions have been picking on Elsie. Now she is feeling sad about her big lovely ears and long trunk. Can you believe it? I think she's beautiful!"

Jon stared at Elsie and said, "WHAT? Elsie, I *love* your long trunk! I wish *I* had such a perfect nose! I can't believe you would think such a bad thing about yourself! Look at me and my enormously long neck! Everyone is always looking up at me and gossiping about me. I hate it!"

All three friends were looking in the pond, deep in thought about their less-than-perfect bodies, when their pal Andy the antelope joined them.

Not knowing what was wrong, Andy excitedly asked, "Would you three like to play with my friends and me? We want to play a game of kickball, but we don't have enough players. It will be fun, and all of you look like you need some cheering up."

Sadly, Elsie answered, "No, thank you. I just don't feel up to it. I'm not that happy today."

"Why not? What's up?" asked Andy.

Elsie, Zol, and Jon told Andy about the mean lions and about how bad they made Elsie feel.

Then Elsie said, "I hate my long trunk and gigantic ears. I've got those lions picking on me all the time, and now all of us are feeling sad about the way we look." Zol and Jon nodded their heads as Elsie continued, "Zol doesn't like her stripes and wants to be one color, and Jon feels like everyone is staring at his long neck. We just want to look normal!"

Andy looked at them questioningly, "NORMAL? What's that? There is no such thing as normal. We are all different. That's what makes us each who we are. We are all very different and interesting animals, no matter what shape, size, or color we come in."

Jon looked confused as he asked, "So what are you saying, Andy? We are all normal, even though we think we're not?"

Andy smiled and said, "All of you are looking at the things you DON'T like about yourselves. But what about all the things you *do* like? It seems to me that none of you are thinking about the good things!"

Andy looked straight at Elsie and said, "Look at the good qualities of your ears and trunk. You have ears that can be used as fans to cool yourself off. And you have a really long trunk, which can be used to pick things up off the ground and reach high places. I know a lot of animals who would love to be you with those ears and that trunk!"

Elsie listened to Andy. Then she smiled as she said, "You are right! I am really lucky."

Then Andy looked at Jon and said, "You have the ability to see everything from way up high, and you can reach really high places."

Next, Andy look at Zol and said, "Zol, you are lucky to be two colors. Most animals are only one color. You have the most beautiful coat of any animal."

Jon and Zol grinned shyly. "You are absolutely right, Andy," they said. "It is okay for us to be different. It makes us who we are."

Jon continued, "Why, I couldn't be a giraffe if I didn't have such a long neck." And Zol said, "I never knew other animals wanted to be like me."

Elsie gazed at her friends proudly as she summed up what Andy had said. "I understand now. There is no such thing as normal. We are all different. We act different and look different." Then, to everyone's surprise, Elsie started flapping her ears confidently. "I'm happy to be an elephant with this great body," she said. "I wouldn't change it for the world."

Elsie, Zol, Jon, and Andy started laughing. "Now that everyone's feeling better," Andy announced, "it's time to play. Come on, everyone, my friends are waiting. They love to meet new and interesting animals. Just like the three of you!"

Elsie, Zol, Jon, and Andy walked toward the grassland, smiling and happy about their conversation. Elsie waved her ears and held her head high, and Zol and Jon walked proudly by her side!

DISCUSSION QUESTIONS

1. Why do you think the lions picked on Elsie? *(They picked on Elsie because she was different.)*

2. Why do you think kids pick on other kids? *(They pick on them because they are different.)*

3. What could Elsie do to stop the lions from teasing her? *(She could ignore them, walk away, or use any other bully-busting technique.)*

4. What can you do if you are being teased? *(You can ignore the teasing, walk away, get help, or use any other bully-busting technique.)*

5. Is there a part of your body or something about yourself that you do not like? *(Accept any appropriate answers.)* Think about the good things about yourself and your body.

6. What can you do to make yourself feel better when you're feeling sad about something? *(You can think positive thoughts. Accept any other appropriate answers.)*

FOLLOW-UP ACTIVITIES

1. **Elsie And The Animals:** Reproduce *Elsie And The Animals* (page 91) for each student. Distribute a copy of the activity sheet and a red and blue crayon to each student. Then review the directions with the students and have them complete the activity sheet. When everyone has competed the activity sheet, have the students tell what choices they made and why they made them.

2. **Encouraging Statements:** Divide the students into pairs. Identify one person in each pair as the "talker" and the other as the "listener." Begin by telling the talker to state one thing he/she does not like about his/her body. The listener should then reply by saying something good about what the talker is unhappy with. For example, the talker could say, "I wish I did not have any freckles." And the listener could reply, "But freckles are cute." Have the pairs join together into groups of four. Then have the listeners relate what they heard the talkers say and their replies. Then have the groups of four become groups of eight and repeat the process. When you have finished this activity, ask several students how they felt when they kept hearing someone say something good about something that had made them feel bad.

ELSIE AND THE ANIMALS

Directions: Below are pictures of each of the animals in the story. There is also a list of character traits. Using a blue crayon, draw a line from each positive character trait to the animal or animals to whom it pertains. Using a red crayon, draw a line from each negative character trait to the animal or animals to whom it pertains. When you have finished, be prepared to explain the reasons for your choices to the group.

Caring

Tolerant

Friendly

Bullying

Teasing

Self-Confident

Leader

Fair

Respectful

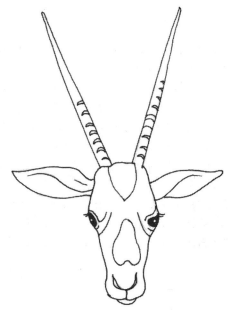

LITTLE LARRY LINKERTON
GRADES 1-3

MANNERS
SPEAKING TOO LOUDLY

WRITTEN BY WANDA S. COOK

Wanda Cook, a counselor in Texas, dedicates this story to the students at Thomas B. Francis Elementary School. She is also a contributor to the book *Special Situations,* published by Mar*co Products.

MAR*CO PRODUCTS, INC. © 2002 1-800-448-2197

LITTLE LARRY LINKERTON

Little Larry Linkerton
Was as tiny as can be.
And yet by far more clever
Than most others from Room 3.

Seemed all the children liked him,
As did Bobby, Bette, and Brad.
But Larry had a problem
That nearly drove them mad!

It happened first one Tuesday morn
While at the city zoo.
When Larry got separated from the class
And didn't know what to do.

Now, this cute little guy was frightened.
For since he is quite small,
He feared no one would see him
Or hear him call at all.

Then this clever little guy
Decided what to do.
He closed his eyes, took one deep breath,
And counted up to 2.

Then suddenly a sound rang out
Like the boom of 50 drums,
The roar of 40 lions,
The bang of 30 guns,

20 thunderous stallions,
And 10 symbols loud and shiny.
It all came from the mouth of Larry,
So cute, so clever, so tiny.

A noise so loud it blew away
The flowers and the trees.
And everyone within the crowd
Was knocked down to their knees.

All the children from his class
And those within the crowd
Clenched their teeth and covered their ears,
Crying, **"Larry, don't be so LOUD!"**

Then Little Larry Linkerton
Would smile in a bashful way.
"I needed your attention," said he,
"To say what I had to say."

"I didn't mean to rattle you.
I'm really not that kind.
But I was lost and I was scared,
And the class I had to find."

But later of his escapade
Larry grew quite proud
Of how **he** got the attention
Of **everyone** in the crowd.

So he tried his little trick again
Twice the next afternoon.
First time, during math drill
And then in the Language Room.

Then that lively little lad
Yes, Larry from Room 3,
Caused a big commotion
In the school's new library.

Instead of the usual story time,
Today they played a game.
To find one student from the class
All 50 states to name.

Last week, the kind librarian
Announced that the lucky winner
Would be the proud owner of
The New Ultimate Super Spinner

Now Larry was determined
That awesome prize to claim.
So he studied hard and he did learn
Each state and its capital by name.

The game rules were quite simple.
The student first to say
All 50 states **when called upon**
Was the winner of the day.

Now Larry knew the answers,
But his hand the librarian could not see
For the bigger hands did hide his hand,
Since was quite tiny.

And after 20 minutes or more
Of playing this simple game,
Not one student from Larry's class
All 50 states could name.

It seemed no one had worked as hard
As Little Larry had.
Not even his friends from the class
Like Bobby, Bette, and Brad.

The librarian would give it one last try
Before the game she'd have to end.
So Larry frantically waved his hand,
As did Gregory B. A. Friend.

Now the librarian saw Gregory's hand,
But Larry's she did not see.
Since Little Larry Linkerton's hand
Is so very, very tiny.

And when she granted Gregory
A chance to win the toy,
Little Larry Linkerton
Was a most unhappy boy.

Then suddenly a sound rang out
Like the boom of 50 drums,
The roar of 40 lions,
The bang of 30 guns,

20 thunderous stallions,
And 10 symbols loud and shiny.
It all came from the mouth of Larry,
So cute, so clever, so tiny.

A noise so loud it could blow away
The flowers and the trees.
And all of those around him
Were knocked down to their knees.

Then the children from his class
And others in the crowd
Clenched their teeth and covered their ears,
Crying, **"Larry don't be so LOUD!"**

The principal came charging in
With the teacher from Room 3,
To discover the school-wide earthquake
was none other than Larry.

Now after meeting with his mom
They designed the perfect plan
To get Little Larry noticed
With just a flicker of his tiny hand.

They agreed that when Larry
Had something he'd like to tell,
He'd raise his hand (and not his voice)
And ring his special bell.

The next week during library time,
Larry rang that bell
And the names of all 50 states
He was first to tell.

Hurray for Little Larry Linkerton!
He was declared official winner
Of the brand new, bright red, shiny,
Ultimate Super Spinner.

And never again did they hear
The boom of 50 drums,
The roar of 40 lions,
The bang of 30 guns,

20 thunderous stallions,
And 10 symbols loud and shiny,
Coming from the mouth of Larry,
So cute, so clever, so tiny.

A noise so loud it blew away
The flowers and the trees.
And everyone within the crowd
Was knocked down to their knees.

And all the children from his class
And those within the crowd
Are very proud of Larry,
Who's learned not to be so

L
O
U
D!

DISCUSSION QUESTIONS

1. Describe Little Larry Linkerton. *(He was very small, smaller than the rest of his classmates.)*

2. What was Larry's big problem? *(He was so little that no one could see him.)*

3. Do you know anyone with the same problem Larry has? How are Larry and that person alike? How are they different? *(Accept any appropriate answers.)*

4. How was Larry feeling at the zoo? *(He felt frightened.)*

5. How did Larry feel after he caused that big fuss? *(He felt proud.)*

6. How did everyone react to Larry's loudness? *(They clenched their teeth and covered their ears.)*

7. Why didn't the librarian call on Larry? *(She could not see him because he was so small.)*

8. What happened when the librarian called on Gregory instead of Larry? *(Larry called out in his loud, loud voice.)*

9. How was Larry helped? *(He was given a special bell to ring when he wanted to speak.)*

10. What happened at the end of the story? *(Larry learned not to be so loud.)*

SUPPLEMENTARY ACTIVITY

1. **Appropriate Voice Levels:** Reproduce *Understanding School-Appropriate Voice Levels* (page 97) for each student. Distribute a copy of the activity sheet; a red, yellow, and green crayon; and a pencil to each student. Review the directions and have the students complete the activity sheet. When everyone has finished, have the students share their answers with the group.

UNDERSTANDING SCHOOL-APPROPRIATE VOICE LEVELS

Directions: Read each question below and write your answers in the spaces provided.

1. Name places at school where it is all right to use a loud voice or an outside-school voice.

   _____

   _____

2. When should you use a more quiet voice or an inside-school voice?

   _____

   _____

3. Is there ever a time you should whisper at school? Why or why not?

   _____

   _____

4. What are some ways that others could remind you if you are not using the appropriate voice?

   _____

   _____

Directions: Underline in red crayon if it is all right to use an outside voice. Underline in yellow crayon if you should use an inside voice. Underline in green crayon if you should whisper.

oral reading time	asking a question	in the library
on the playground	walking in the halls	in the cafeteria
during recess	during gym time	in the front office
at the water fountain	in the restroom	on the school bus
when the teacher is out of the classroom		walking home from school
asking the teacher a question during an important test		

BOTHERSOME BUGS
GRADES 2-3

SELF-DISCIPLINE
FOCUSING
PAYING ATTENTION

WRITTEN BY PATRICIA PETTY

Patricia Petty is an elementary counselor in Tennessee.

BOTHERSOME BUGS

Lisa Ladybug let out a sigh.
Without hearing, she couldn't learn.
She struggled to listen carefully
So she could answer at her turn.

But sitting near Cindy Centipede
Made listening really hard.
Cindy tapped her feet—and her feet—and her feet
Until Lisa's nerves felt overly jarred.

Lisa tuned out Cindy's tapping,
Thinking only about the math.
By focusing on her teacher
She kept her mind on the right path.

Adam Ant was studying science
When he jumped with a start.
His notes went flying on the floor
The loud bang sped up his heart.

Jamie June Bug was the culprit
When he decided to fly from the room.
The wind made by his flapping wings
Slammed the door with a loud BOOM!

Adam said to his heart,
"Slow down! It's OK.
I just hope that this room
Stays calm the rest of the day."

Sam Spider was trying to learn
To write cursive letters with a pen.
And was having great difficulty
With the letters *m* and *n.*

Marcus Mosquito sat next to Sam,
And his long nose sniffed all day.
Each sniff bugged Sam more and more,
And his pen went every which way.

Finally, Sam Spider just had to ask
"May I please move my seat?
If I keep sitting in this spot
My work will never be very neat."

Harry Hopper listened and learned
From the video about green plants.
He really was interested and wanted to hear,
But Ben Bee kept talking to the ants.

If Harry ever wanted to learn
The facts about the plants,
He had to decide to make up his mind
To ignore the noise made by the ants.

Harry concentrated with all his might,
His eyes locked on the screen.
He tuned his ears into the facts
And remembered what he had seen.

Looking at all the assignments,
Brianne Beetle had much work to do.
Mr. Fly was keeping them busy today.
Boardwork, worksheets, and coloring, too!

Brianne got tired of moving her pencil.
Her eyes began to look around.
She spied colors by the windowsill,
Moving, dancing, flitting up and down!

The butterflies that were fluttering by
Reminded her of the coloring sheet
She had to get busy and finish
To get the teacher's promised treat.

And so our little poem
Shows that even bugs can be harassed.
But these bugs said good-bye to bugging,
And paid attention to their tasks.

DISCUSSION QUESTIONS

1. Why was it hard for Lisa Ladybug to listen to the teacher? *(Cindy Centipede was tapping her feet.)* What did Lisa do to help herself be a good listener? *(She ignored the irritating noises and concentrated on what was being taught.)*

2. Adam Ant was scared by a loud noise. How did he help himself feel better? *(He told his heart it was OK.)*

3. What was Sam Spider trying to do? *(He was trying to learn cursive writing.)* What did he ask his teacher? *(He asked if he could move his seat.)*

4. What was making it hard for Harry Hopper to pay attention to the video? *(Ben Bee kept talking to the ants.)* What did Harry do about this problem? *(He concentrated with all his might and tuned out the noises.)*

5. Brianne Beetle had a hard time sticking to her tasks. What distracted her? *(The butterflies outside the window distracted her.)* What got her back on track? *(The colorful butterflies reminded her of the coloring she had to do.)*

6. We all get distracted by things that bother us. What are some distractions that you have to deal with? *(Accept any appropriate answers.)*

7. What do you say to yourself when you are trying to ignore distractions? *(Accept any appropriate answers.)*

SUPPLEMENTARY ACTIVITY

1. **Bothersome Bugs**: Reproduce *Bothersome Bugs* (page 102) for each student. Distribute a copy of the activity sheet and a pencil to each student. Review the directions and tell the students how much time they have to complete the activity. When the allotted time has elapsed, have the students share their answers with the group.

BOTHERSOME BUGS

List some of the bothersome "bugs" that you try to ignore:

_____

_____

_____

_____

When you ignore the bothersome "bugs" you can pay more attention to important matters. List some of the these important matters.

_____

_____

_____

_____

CHARACTER-EDUCATION STORIES

CHARACTER-TRAIT STORIES
EMPHASIZING
RELATIONSHIPS WITH OTHERS

PLAYING WITH PATIENCE
GRADES 2-4

UNDERSTANDING DIFFERENCES
PATIENCE

WRITTEN BY SHELLY ARNESON

Shelly Arneson is an elementary counselor in Florida.

PLAYING WITH PATIENCE

With his feet propped up on his green backpack, Rusty frantically pressed buttons on his videogame. "Oh, no! I lost again!" he complained to no one in particular. The airport was busy with the rush of morning travelers. Rusty's sandy brown hair lay matted to his head, and he brushed it distractedly off his face. He was worried about his Gramma Rose.

"Gramma Rose had a stroke," Rusty's mom had told him last week. "We need to go to Phoenix to see her." Rusty hadn't really understood what a stroke was, so his mom had explained that the stroke had affected Gramma Rose's brain. She couldn't move her left side any more and she might never be able to move again. She would have to learn lots of things all over again, including how to do simple tasks around the house that she had always done.

"How will Gramma Rose play *Tomb Raider* with me if she can't move her left hand?" Rusty asked, staring at his videogame. His mom laughed softly and replied, "Rusty, Gramma never played videogames *before* her stroke." She tousled his hair, and then turned back to the book she was reading.

Rusty yawned a great, cavernous yawn and then leaned over to quiz his dad, "How much longer until we get on the plane?" Before his dad could answer, the gate attendant tapped the microphone and announced a 30-minute flight delay. Rusty groaned, "Oh, no!"

"Patience, Rusty, is a virtue you might do well to learn," Mom said.

Rusty picked up his game and walked over to the window. He watched a huge airplane land in the distance and thought about Gramma Rose in Phoenix. He would see her soon, and he was scared that she would look strange. What if she didn't talk the same way? Would she still recognize him? He plopped down on the carpet and was soon absorbed in his videogame, jumping over bad guys and hurdling obstacles.

"Hey! *Tomb Raider* is my favorite game," the freckle-faced girl sitting next to him announced. "Could I play for a minute?"

"Sure," mumbled Rusty. "I keep losing, anyway."

As the girl reached over to take the game, she said, "My name is Molly. I'm flying to Arizona to see the Grand Canyon! Thanks for letting me play." It was then that Rusty noticed that Molly had only one arm. There was a small stump near her shoulder where her right arm should be. He watched as she played the game with her left hand, using all her fingers as skillfully as a talented piano player at the keyboard. She didn't seem to be bothered by having only one of her arms and one of her hands.

Rusty couldn't help himself. He had to ask, "How did you learn to play … like that?" Before she could answer, Molly shouted a loud "Yes!" as she beat the game.

"I wanted to play videogames. But when I first tried to play, I kept messing up," Molly told Rusty. "I had to really work hard to learn to do this."

"But, gosh, you play better than I do!" Rusty said in amazement.

"Well, I guess that could be true," Molly smiled, "but it's not easy to play with one hand. I have to be really patient. It took me a long time to get used to being patient, but I've gotten used to it now."

A few minutes later, the gate attendant announced their flight to Phoenix was boarding. Molly and Rusty exchanged e-mail addresses and promised to send each other the names of their favorite games.

"Why don't you send me some tips on beating this one, too?" Rusty asked.

Molly laughed and agreed, turning off the game and holding it out to Rusty. Rusty took back his videogame, said goodbye to Molly, and boarded the flight with his parents. He settled in his seat and fastened the belt around his waist. He stared at his videogame and thought about Molly and Gramma Rose. Gramma Rose might have to learn how to do some things all over again, but Rusty decided he was glad they were going to Phoenix. He would help teach her what she needed to know. All it would take was a little patience.

 MAR*CO PRODUCTS, INC. © 2002 1-800-448-2197

DISCUSSION QUESTIONS

1. How were Gramma Rose and Molly alike? *(Molly had to learn to do things without the use of her arm and Gramma Rose was going to have to learn to do things without the use of her left side.)*

2. In what ways does Molly have to be patient in her daily life? *(Molly has to be patient when learning to do anything that would ordinarily require a right hand or arm.)*

3. How did Molly teach Rusty about patience? *(Rusty learned that the reason Molly played the videogame so well was because she had had the patience to take the time to learn how to play it with one hand.)*

4. What are some ways that you can demonstrate patience at home? At school? With friends? *(Accept any appropriate answers.)*

FOLLOW-UP ACTIVITIES

1. **Non-Dominant Hand:** Distribute a grade-level-appropriate word search and a pencil to each student. Tell the students they are to find five words as quickly as they can, writing only with their non-dominant hand. When everyone has finished, discuss how frustrating it can be when such an easy task becomes a challenge.

2. **Similarities And Differences:** Have each student choose a partner. Tell the students they are to work with their partners to list as many ways as they can think of to show how the two of them are alike and how they are different from one another. When every pair of partners has finished the exercise, have each pair name one similarity and one difference that they found. To make the activity more challenging, tell the students that once a similarity or difference has been mentioned, it may not be used again.

LITTLE WILLIE'S LESSON
GRADES 1-3

SHARING
CARING

WRITTEN BY WANDA S. COOK

Wanda Cook is an elementary counselor in Texas. She is a contributor to *Special Situations*, published by Mar✳co Products.

LITTLE WILLIE'S LESSON

This story is about Little Willie,
A tiny tot 'bout the age of four,
Whose bashful smile and innocent eyes
I'm certain you will adore.

Not only is this chap charming,
But he's a most fortunate boy.
For his school-tray is stacked, and that is a fact,
With every imaginable toy!

Willie's toys were Willie's and *only* Willie's toys,
His classmates could but sit, wish, and stare.
And how he'd quiver and shake when his teacher, Ms. Blake,
Would ask him his toys to share.

"But, please, Ms. Blake," Willie pleaded,
When she made her humble request.
"This is Willie's school-tray with Willie's school toys.
Don't make Willie share with the rest."

"These are Willie's toys,"
He continued to say
In his charming and
Innocent kind of a way.

"This is Willie's ball
And Willie's bat.
This is Willie's toy doggie
And Willie's toy cat.

"These are Willie's skates
That zoom real fast,
And Willie's toy soldier,
Colonel Billy McBlast.

"This is Willie's Mr. Muscle
And Willie's football team."
His list went on and on
Forever, it seemed.

"This is Willie's Slinky
And Willie's kite.
And to make Willie share
Just wouldn't be right.

"This is Willie's castle
And Willie's moat.
This is Willie's truck
And Willie's boat.

"This is Willie's fire engine
And Willie's videogame.
See here on this tray?
It says Willie's name.

"Not Daryl or Ben
Or Joseph or Royce.
Not Karen or Dede
Or Keeta or Joyce.

"Not Sam or John-Michael,
Steve or Simone.
But *Willie's* name
And *Willie's* alone!

"So please don't make
Willie quiver and shake,"
He said, turning his attention
Back to Ms. Blake.

" 'Cause Willie has tried
So hard to explain
That these are Willie's toys
And this is Willie's name."

"Have it your way, Willie,"
Sighed his teacher, Ms. Blake.
"I will never again
Make you quiver and shake.

"By asking you to share
Your collection of toys
With the other girls
Or with the other boys."

Then she knelt down beside him
With a hug and a smile.
"You may get quite lonely
After a while,

"When your classmates
No longer sit, wish, and stare,
Or ask you your collection
Of toys to share."

But Willie seemed happy
As he played alone,
Without Sam or John-Michael,
Steve or Simone.

Without Karen, Dede,
Keeta, or Joyce,
Without Daryl and Ben,
Joseph or Royce!

The next day came
And the day after that,
Still no one came near Willie
Next to him no one sat.

No one asked for his Slinky
Or for his kite,
'Cause Willie himself
Said that wouldn't be right.

Then suddenly Willie was no longer happy.
He felt sad and all alone.
So, he took his school-tray to share and to play
With John-Michael, Steve, and Simone.

"No, thanks, Willie,"
Said each of the boys.
"We now have our
Own collection of toys."

"Then I'll share," said Willie,
"With Keeta and Joyce.
I'll share with Karen,
Ben, Joseph, and Royce."

But Willie's classmates
All said the same.
"No, thank you. We have
Our own special game."

So there stood Willie
With his ball and his bat,
His little toy doggie,
And his little toy cat.

His tiny skates
That zoom real fast,
And his favorite toy soldier,
Colonel Billy McBlast.

His Mr. Muscle,
His football team.
This list goes on
And on it seems.

His red fire engine
And his videogame.
Right there in that tray
That says Willie's name.

Willie stood there
With his castle and moat.
He stood there
With his truck and his boat.

He stood there
Sad and all alone,
Without Joseph, John-Michael,
Steve, and Simone.

Without Daryl, Keeta,
Dede, and Joyce.
Without Sam, Karen,
Ben, or Royce.

Then slowly he walked
To the desk of Ms. Blake,
And promised he'd never
Again quiver and shake.

If she asked, he would
Share his collection of toys
With the other girls
And the other boys.

And never again
Was he all alone,
Without Joseph, the girls,
the boys—Simone.

'Cause Willie,
This tiny tot of 'bout four
Whose smile and eyes
We all adore

Found out that when
We learn to share,
It shows how much
We truly care!

DISCUSSION QUESTIONS

1. What was Willie's problem? *(He did not want to share his toys.)*

2. Why do you think it was so hard for him to share with others? *(Accept any appropriate answers.)*

3. How did the children in Willie's class feel about him? How do you think they felt when he wouldn't share? *(Accept any appropriate answers.)*

4. How did his teacher, Ms. Blake, feel about him? *(She liked him.)* How do you know? *(She hugged him and smiled.)*

5. Do you know anyone like Willie? *(Accept only yes or no answers. Do not allow the students to mention any names.)*

6. Have you ever been selfish? *(Accept any appropriate answers.)*

7. Has anyone ever been selfish with you? How did it make you feel? *(Allow only yes or no answers and an expression of feelings. Do not allow the students to mention any names.)*

8. How did Ms. Blake and the students in Willie's class help him? *(Ms. Blake did not force him to share his toys. The students in his class ignored him. When these two things took place, Willie realized he did not have any friends.)*

9. How did Willie feel when no one wanted to play with him? *(He felt lonely and sad.)*

10. Did Willie learn his lesson? Do you think he now understands how the students felt when he wouldn't share with them? How do you know? *(Yes. Yes. He went to Ms. Blake and told her he would share with the other students.)*

SUPPLEMENTARY ACTIVITY

1. **Learning When To Share:** Reproduce *Learning When To Share* (page 115) for each student. Distribute a copy of the activity sheet and a pencil or crayons to each student. Read the directions with the students and tell them how much time they have to complete the activity. When the allotted time has elapsed, have the students share their answers with the group. Compliment correct answers and correct incorrect ones.

Name _____

LEARNING WHEN TO SHARE

Directions: Draw a happy face ☺ beside the statement if it is true. Draw a sad face ☹ beside the statement if it is false.

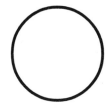

1. Sharing your things with others shows that you care.

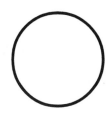

2. Since sharing shows that we care, it is OK to share answers with a friend during a spelling test.

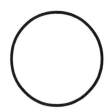

3. If you have two pencils, and your classmate needs one, you should share.

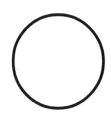

4. If your friend forgets her toothbrush when spending the night at your house, it is OK to share yours with her.

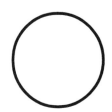

5. If a classmate wants a sip of your milk, it is OK to let him have a very small sip.

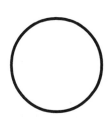

6. If you find a wallet on the playground, you should share the money with all of your friends except the ones who never share with you.

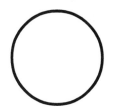

7. Your principal is very kind, so it is OK to share your mom's new diamond ring with her.

SNEEZE IN THREES
GRADES 3-5

BULLYING
FORGIVENESS

WRITTEN BY PAMELA WIDMANN

Pamela Widmann is an educator in Colorado. She teaches through storytelling and dramatics. At present, she is the program assistant for her district's gifted and talented program.

SNEEZE IN THREES

"This day stinks!" Jamie screamed, as he left the house in a hurry. BANG! He slammed the door behind him so loudly that he didn't hear what his mother called to him.

She always said the same things, anyhow. Things like, "You should have gotten up when the alarm rang," or "Didn't you hear me calling you?"

"Whatever!" thought Jamie as he jumped through the closing yellow doors of the bus.

He had gotten up late, his bubblegum toothpaste squirted all over the counter, his favorite shirt with the blue stripes on the sleeves was dirty, AND he didn't have time for breakfast. Jamie LOVED breakfast—sugar-coated, multicolored cereal with funny boxes to hide behind so he didn't have to LOOK at his stupid brother. Even worse, there was a spelling test today! The test was on a word list he'd lost two days before. One of the words on the spelling list was *forgiveness.*

"Why would I want to know how to spell a word I don't even like and will never use in my WHOLE LIFE?" Jamie wondered.

Mornings used to be fun. Jamie's father used to sing him awake, but that was before his father had moved to a different house. Jamie's mom used to have cereal waiting for him in his special bowl, the one with the picture of an alien on the bottom. But now she was too busy getting ready for her new job to do that in the morning.

"Mornings stink!" Jamie mumbled as he pushed those thoughts out of his mind.

"AH CHOOOO!" Jamie sneezed on the bus. "AH CHOOO!" he sneezed again. And then there was silence. SILENCE!

"Where's my third sneeze?" Jamie panicked. "I ALWAYS sneeze in threes. Dad says EVERYONE sneezes in threes."

Jamie wiggled his pug nose in circles, trying to find the tickle. He stared at the sun and dropped his mouth open. NOTHING! Then he noticed Zach and Bailey watching him from the next seat. They were laughing at his silly faces and scrunched-up nose, so he punched them. He punched them both. What happened next was school bus history.

Bailey and Zach cried and told the bus driver what Jamie had done. So as soon as Jamie got to school, he was told to report to the principal's office. This was the third time in a week that Jamie had been sent to the principal.

"Jamie, why did you hit the other children on the bus this morning?" asked Mrs. Guzzy, the principal. "Is everything OK?"

"Yeah, it's OK," Jamie answered. "They were laughing at me. They started it. I didn't even hit them hard. And anyway, mornings stink. Did you ever sneeze only twice?"

"Jamie, this is the third time you have been to see me this week, and I don't think it has anything to do with sneezes," Mrs. Guzzy said. "It's time to call your parents." Mrs. Guzzy had Jamie's phone card in her hand.

"Good luck with THAT information!" grumbled Jamie. "Mom has a new job and Dad lives in another house." Then Jamie handed her the crumpled phone number he carried in his pocket every day.

"Thank you, Jamie. Now why don't you go back to class? I'll call for you later. I expect you to find another way to express your frustrations. In the meantime, there are consequences for your behavior. I'll discuss this with your parents and your teacher. No recess until further notice," Mrs. Guzzy said. Then she stood. Jamie knew that was his cue to stand, too.

As he turned to leave, Mrs. Guzzy said sweetly, "I only sneeze in threes. Doesn't everybody?"

These words may have been meant to lighten things up, but Jamie knew now that his day, maybe his week, maybe his WHOLE LIFE was going to STINK forever because he had lost a sneeze on the bus.

The next morning, Jamie was back in the principal's office with his mom and dad. He couldn't believe they had scheduled this torture in the MORNING when they knew how he felt about mornings! Jamie's mom and dad sat very far apart in the very small office.

Jamie didn't really hear what was being said. He was mostly watching the movement of his shoestring over the floor vent in Mrs. Guzzy's office. Besides, looking at the grown-ups only reminded him of the arguing and yelling that had filled his ears in the last year or so. But the grown-ups kept looking at HIM while they were talking.

"Just leave me alone!" he finally yelled when they asked another question he didn't even hear.

It was decided, as grown-ups decide things all the time about kids and their free time, that Jamie was to meet a new grown-up to learn about stuff that wasn't in his schoolbooks.

"Oh, brother," Jamie sighed. Then he thought, "I wonder how many times this new grown-up sneezes ..."

The next day, Jamie went to his first meeting with the new grown-up. As Jamie barreled into the meeting room, the other kids said, "Yuck, it's Jamie! Do we have to have HIM in our group, Ms. Flipper? He shoves and punches everybody."

 MAR✳CO PRODUCTS, INC. © 2002 1-800-448-2197

As for Jamie, he was happy to be there. After all, he got to leave his regular class, which, at that moment, happened to be *art*. "Art stinks," Jamie thought. He said that because he wished he could draw as well as the other kids. Jamie had always wanted to be able to draw dinosaurs, but he just scribbled so no one would laugh if his dinosaur looked like a blob or something.

Weeks and months passed, and Jamie began to learn from his special class. He learned how much he missed his parents being in the same house. He learned he didn't miss the arguing and yelling. He actually cried once, in front of those kids, and NOBODY laughed.

Jamie began to understand why he felt angry a lot, and Ms. Flipper gave him new things to do and words to say when he felt like hitting or shoving someone. Sometimes Jamie forgot. But most of the time, he really *was* changing.

"Wake up! Wake up!" yelled Jamie's new alarm from beneath the covers. Jamie's mom had bought him a new stuffed ball that had an alarm clock hidden inside. It yelled and jumped around the bed when it was time for him to get up.

"That alarm clock was the BEST idea ever, Mom!" he yelled as he slid down the painted railing to the kitchen for breakfast.

"And we still have some Fruit Nuggets cereal left! This morning doesn't even stink," Jamie said, smiling, as he placed the box on the table directly between him and his little brother.

"Ah choo!" sneezed his little brother. "Ah choo! Ah choo!" He sneezed two more times.

"That's three," thought Jamie, suddenly losing his enthusiasm and remembering his bad luck. It had been months since he had sneezed. He wondered if the next time he sneezed, he would sneeze only once as a third sneeze OR if the count of his sneezes would be messed up FOREVER!

The bus was extra-full that morning, because they had to share with another route whose bus had had gas trouble. The kids were all laughing about THAT bus! When Jamie got on the bus, there was nowhere to sit—nowhere except next to those whiners, Bailey and Zach.

Jamie tried to squish next to Bob. But Bob shoved him back into the aisle just as the driver said, "Take your seat!"

Jamie could feel the frustration and anger building inside him like the sound of the bus engine as it pushed forward. He tried to think of Ms. Flipper's ideas. He tried to remember his parents' advice. But NO WAY did he want to sit by those kids who had told on him so many times before. He tried to squat in the aisle and not be noticed. But the driver had one of those magic mirrors and yelled to the back, "Jamie! Sit down! There's a seat on your left just a few rows back."

"Oh, boy!" thought Jamie. "Here goes ..."

He turned with a scowl and prepared to say something mean like he used to do. Something like, "Move your butts, jerks! I gotta sit down." But as he turned, he saw Bailey and Zach motioning and scootching over to give him the best spot by the window. Was he imagining this? Weren't they scared of him or mad at him or laughing at him or ... ANYTHING?

Bailey and Zach had talked with each other many times about feeling angry at Jamie. They sort of wanted to be mean to him, to get even for all the times Jamie had been mean to them. Sometimes they even planned things to do to Jamie to hurt his feelings. And they had laughed when their friends said bad things about Jamie. But Jamie hadn't picked on them for quite a while. And when they saw his face after Bob shoved him, they knew how he felt. He looked just like they did when they felt embarrassed or hurt.

Zach and Bailey looked at each other before Jamie turned toward them. They knew they would feel better about themselves if they were nice to him. They thought, "Why not give him a chance?"

"Here, Jamie, there's plenty of room," Bailey said as she smiled at him.

Jamie didn't say anything. He just sat down, wondering what planet he had landed on.

"Want some?" Zach asked as he offered Jamie a piece of his strawberry fruit tart.

Jamie didn't answer. He didn't know what to say.

So he turned to look out the window and think about what had just happened. Then a word popped into his mind. The word was *forgiveness*. Yep! The word he'd thought he'd never use was now a word he truly understood. Jamie decided it was his new favorite word and smiled warmly at his new friends.

As the bus pulled to a stop in front of the school, Jamie suddenly felt a twitch ...

no, a tingle ...

no, an itch!

"AHCHOOOOOOO!" sneezed Jamie.

He stood up and spread his arms wide, waiting to see what would happen next. His eyes were bulging with anticipation and his mouth was open in suspense.

The kids all got quiet and watched him with curiosity. The half-chewed fruit tart sat precariously on his teeth. Seconds, that felt like hours, passed! Jamie wondered if this was the third sneeze he had been waiting for OR if more sneezes were about to happen.

Suddenly, something broke the silence. A sound from nowhere. An explosive, unexpected, tension-splitting sound. It was the sound of Zach politely saying, "Bless you."

DISCUSSION QUESTIONS

1. Who was the bully in the story? *(Jamie was the bully.)*

2. How do you know he was the bully? *(He punched and picked on kids, especially Zach and Bailey.)*

3. What seemed to be the main cause of Jamie's problem? *(His parents were separated.)*

4. Are your problems an excuse for bullying? Why or why not? *(No. Accept any appropriate answers.)*

5. Who was Ms. Flipper, and what did she do? *(Ms. Flipper was the school counselor, and she taught him ways, other than hitting and shoving, to handle his anger.)*

6. What was the first reaction of the other students when they saw Jamie was to be in their group? *(They were upset, because they thought he would ruin their group.)*

7. How did the schoolbus having gas trouble help Jamie? *(He had to sit with Zach and Bailey and he learned they were nice kids after all.)*

8. How did the title, *Sneeze In Threes* fit into the story? *(In the beginning of the story, Jamie sneezed only twice. This bothered him, because he always thought there should be three sneezes. In the end, when he was sitting with Zach and Bailey, he finally had his third sneeze.)*

9. What did Zach and Bailey do when they asked Jamie to sit by them? *(They forgave him for his past behavior and gave him a second chance.)*

SUPPLEMENTARY ACTIVITY

1. **Forgiveness Or No?:** Ask the students to name different bullying behaviors. Write their answers on the chalkboard. When the students have finished naming bullying behaviors, ask them to vote, by raising their hands, whether each behavior listed should be forgiven. If the majority says the behavior should be forgiven, write an "F" beside the action. If most of the students feel the behavior should *not* be forgiven, leave the space beside the behavior blank. When the students have voted on each behavior, have them justify their answers.

P.J., PLEASE!
GRADES 3-5

PERSONAL SPACE
FEELINGS
RESPECT
FRIENDSHIP

WRITTEN BY DARLENE PULLIAM

Darlene Pulliam is a guidance counselor in Fairfax County, Virginia. She is the author of *Toby, The Test-Taking Toucan*, available from Mar*co Products, Inc.

P.J., PLEASE!

"P. J., please ...." Oh, no! Not again! Why does my teacher, Ms. Peggy Parrot, always say, "P. J., please? Why does she always look so **sad** when she has to stop teaching and say my name? Why does she sometimes come over and perch next to me? Why do I always get in trouble? Why do the other parrots in class look at me? Why me? What did I do?

My name is P. J. Parrot and this is my story. I'm so **excited**. I'm finally old enough to go to Rain Forest School. My brother, Teddy, went to school last year. He told me about all the new things I would learn at school. I felt so grown-up and **proud**. I just knew my beak would grow stronger and my tail feathers would grow longer and become even more colorful. I can hardly wait to start learning and making new friends at school.

On the first day of school, Teddy and I were eating a yummy breakfast of fruit, berries, nuts, and Parrot Fruit Loop Cereal. Teddy was telling me how much fun school would be. I twirled around and did some acrobatics on a nearby limb and screeched loudly, "Teddy, I can't *wait* to go to school! I'm going to learn to do math! I'm going to learn to write! I'm going to be the best reader in my class! I'm going to make *so many* new friends."

I grabbed Teddy roughly and threw my brightly colored wings around him. Teddy's strong claws almost lost their grip on the tree branch as he pulled away from me. I guess Teddy didn't like my rough hug.

Teddy looked **upset** as he flew to our nesting hole high up in a dead tree. I could hardly hear him say, from his hiding place in the tree, "Yes, you will learn many things in school, but P. J., please, you *must* also learn to treat others with respect." Teddy was right.

When I got to school, Ms. Peggy, my teacher, welcomed everyone with her pretty parrot smile. She told us to find a spot to perch on on a tree branch. The she explained our classroom rules about working and playing together, about being respectful, about respecting each other's personal space, and about being good friends with others.

I listened, but I forgot I was in school. I screeched noisily, "WOW! That's a lot of rules to remember!" All the other little parrots looked at me.

I remember something else that happened on the first day of school. I didn't know any other parrots in my class. I saw a little parrot putting together a puzzle in the puzzle center. I wanted to find out his name and be his friend, so I hopped right next to him and screeched loudly in his ear, "I just love puzzles." Guess what else I did?

I hit him on his back. I didn't hit very hard—it was just a little hit. I wonder why he didn't talk with me or tell me his name. He didn't want to play with me, either.

The little parrot looked really **scared**. "Ms. Peggy, I want to go to a different center! I'm **worried** that he will hit me again," he said as he pointed to me. Why was he afraid of me? I didn't mean to scare him. I guess no little parrot wants to be hit, even if it isn't very hard.

Ms. Peggy reminded me that a better way to make friends would be to say, "Hi, may I play in the puzzle center with you. Or may I have a turn when you finish?" She reminded me to use my words, *not* my body, when I want to talk or play with someone.

One day, my classmates were perched on branches in a big circle, listening to a story. I perched next to Tony and did a couple of my favorite acrobatic tricks. He was listening to the story and didn't notice me, so I started leaning against him. Tony moved to the other end of the branch. "P. J., please don't sit so close to me. I'm **uncomfortable** when you lean against me," he said. I guess Tony really didn't want me to lean against him.

Maybe he didn't like my acrobatic tricks, either. Maybe he just wanted to listen to the story.

I'm a very curious little bird, so I wondered what Susie, Billy, and Rosie were building in the block center. Working together and sharing the blocks, they had almost finished building a really tall parrot tree-home. They had even left an open space at the top for the nesting hole. I wanted to help, so I squeezed in beside them. "P. J., please, you're **crowding** us," they said.

Rosie was stacking the last block on top of the tree-home. Oh, no! I bumped Rosie's wing, and all the blocks fell crashing down. "P. J., please, you make me feel so **frustrated**. We worked so hard on this tree-home," Rosie said. "Now look at it! It's ruined." I just wanted to help, and I didn't mean to make their tree-home fall. Now Rosie, Susie, and Billy don't want to be in the block center with me.

 MAR✳CO PRODUCTS, INC. © 2002 1-800-448-2197

So far, school hadn't been much fun for me. On another day, I decided to make friends with Joey. I tapped him on the wing. He kept working and didn't pay any attention to me, so I started touching his school work. "P. J., please don't bother me. Keep your hands to yourself," he said.

Joey hopped to another branch. "Ms. Peggy, P. J. is **annoying** me. I can't do my work," Joey complained. I was only trying to be friendly. Maybe he was more interested in doing his school work than in being my friend.

I had learned many new things in school. Mom and Dad kept telling me, "P. J., you are so smart. You do so well in school." I wondered, why, if I'm so smart, do the other parrots not want to work or play with me? They never choose me to be on their teams. What am I doing wrong?

I love to go to music class, and we take turns being the line-leader. One day, Eddie was the line-leader, and I was next in line behind him. Mr. Macaw, our music teacher, told us we would learn some new calls that parrots in other rain forest neighborhoods use. He explained some of the calls were very noisy. He said we would have fun shrieking and screaming the new calls to some really loud, fun music. I wanted to get to music class as fast as I could.

Can you guess what I did? I gave Eddie a little push. Eddie was trying to be a good line-leader. He wouldn't speed up, so I pushed him again. Eddie got **angry**. "P. J., please stop pushing me. Mr. Macaw, P. J. is pushing me. I don't want to walk next to him anymore." I felt sad when Mr. Macaw reminded me that pushing is not a kind thing for friends to do.

Sometimes, when I want to answer a question in class, I forget to raise my hand. I just scream out my ideas. Ms. Peggy reminds me, "P. J., please remember the rule to raise your hand before you speak. If you don't give others a chance, some little parrots who need more time to think might feel too **shy** or **embarrassed** to answer." I always feel great when I share my ideas. I didn't think about how others feel when I won't listen to them.

I don't want to go to school any more. Every day, I try to remember what Ms. Peggy has taught me. I try to finish all my work. I try to make friends with the other little parrots in my class at Rain Forest School, but something is wrong— really wrong! I haven't made any new friends. Everyone just says, "P. J., please …"

Finally, one day, Ms. Peggy asked me to stay in during recess. "P. J., you seem to be having trouble making friends this year. I think I might be able to help you. Do you remember when we talked about our classroom rules at the beginning of the year? Do you remember what we learned about *personal space?* Do you remember that friends *must* respect each other's *personal space?"*

I really didn't want to miss recess. So at first, I hid my face under my wing. I popped my head out and answered Ms. Peggy in my silliest voice, "Personal space? Oh, I remember. I'm going to ride my *personal space* ship to the moon." I hid my face again and then popped out to ask, "Am I going to outer *space* to look at the stars?" Ms. Peggy said, "P. J., please!" I hid my face and popped out again. "I know, I'm going to get my very own *personal space* station videogame to play in school."

Ms. Peggy really looked serious now. "P. J., you are very smart and have done some excellent schoolwork this year, but ... P. J., please, remember you are *in school*. I know all little parrots love to screech and be noisy. I know you like to play parrot games and do acrobatics. I also know you feel sad when the other parrots won't play with you or choose you to be on their teams. P. J., I would like to help you. It's OK to be noisy and playful in the rain forest, but in school we *must* remember to follow all the rules and respect the *personal space* of others."

"OK, Ms. Peggy. I'm sorry. I just want the others to notice me and be my friend. That's why I act silly and try to get attention. I guess I didn't listen very well the first time you explained about *personal space*. Would you please explain it one more time?" asked P. J.

"All right, P. J., but please listen carefully," Ms. Peggy began. "Our *personal space* includes our body. It is the area around our body where we feel safe, comfortable, and not too crowded. No one has permission to get into anyone's personal space without being invited. Personal space is also the desk or table where we do our schoolwork. It is the space around us when we sit in a circle or walk in line. P. J., you may only need a little bit of personal space, but other parrots may need more personal space in order to feel comfortable and safe. Friends always respect the personal space that each little parrot needs."

Ms. Peggy helped me understand personal space by saying, "P. J., pretend to blow up a balloon. Then pretend you are in the center of the balloon." She explained that the area inside the balloon is my personal space and told me to remember that other little parrots' personal space is the pretend balloon around each of their bodies. Ms. Peggy also explained it another way. She told me to stretch out my wings, tail feathers, and beak, and then turn in a circle. The pretend circle around me is my personal space.

"Wow! I think I get it," I said. "Every little parrot has a *personal space*. I have my own *personal space*, too. I think I have been getting into the other little parrots' personal space too much, and they are not happy. I think I finally know why I haven't made any new friends."

I felt so much better when Ms. Peggy said, "P. J., you really are an intelligent little bird, and I know you will remember what we have talked about. If you forget again, I will remind you. I will give you a signal. Can you help me to think of a signal that we can use?" Now, if I accidentally forget the personal space rule, Ms. Peggy reminds me with our special signal. Then I say, "I'm sorry" to the other little parrot, and I stop getting into his personal space.

I am so glad that Ms. Peggy taught us rules about how to get along with each other and be kind in Rain Forest School. Now I do my very best to remember all the rules, especially the rule to respect everyone's personal space. I have lots of new friends, too. Our classroom is a nice place for all of us to work and learn together. I wake up every morning thinking that I can't wait to go to school. When all the little parrots in my class work hard and remember the rules, we all get along and are **happy**. Best of all, Ms. Peggy and my classmates hardly ever say, "P. J., please ...."

DISCUSSION QUESTIONS

1. What did P. J. always forget that caused Ms. Peggy to say, "P. J. , please …?" *(He forgot to respect the personal space of others.)*

2. What did P. J. do when Ms. Peggy tried to talk with him about personal space? *(He hid his face under his wing and said silly things.)*

3. How did Ms. Peggy explain personal space? *(Our personal space includes our own body. It is also the area around our body where we feel safe, comfortable, and uncrowded. No one has permission to get into anyone's personal space without being invited. Personal space is also the desk or table where we do our school work. It is the space around us when we sit in a circle or walk in line.)*

4. How did Ms. Peggy help P. J. understand personal space? *(She told him to blow up a pretend balloon or think of a pretend circle around him, and they decided on a special signal to remind him when he was invading another student's personal space.)*

5. What were some of the mistakes P. J. made when he got into other parrots' personal space? *(He hugged them too hard, hit, leaned against someone, crowded others, tapped others, touched or destroyed other's work, pushed, shouted out, and did not give others a turn.)*

6. If you were one of the parrots in P. J.'s class, how would you handle it when P. J. got into your personal space? *(Accept any appropriate answers.)*

7. What thoughts do you think P. J. had when he realized none of the other parrots wanted to play with him? *(Accept any appropriate answers.)*

8. What do you think would have happened to P. J. if he had not asked Ms. Peggy for help? *(Accept any appropriate answers.)*

9. How can the lesson P. J. learned help you be a better friend? *(Accept any appropriate answers.)*

10. P. J. learned to be a better friend. How did he act differently at the end of the story? *(He listened, respected others' space, and said, "I'm sorry.")*

FOLLOW-UP ACTIVITIES

1. **Feelings Activity:** Make a chart with feelings words and feelings faces to be matched to the words. The words on the chart should relate to the *P. J., Please!* story. (See the ***bold/italicized*** words in the story.) Then ask the following questions. When a student responds correctly, ask him/her to choose the face and match it to the feeling word on the chart. This can be done by attaching velcro to the back of each feeling face and next to each feeling word on the chart.

    1. How did Ms. Peggy feel when P. J. forgot the class rules? *(sad)*

    2. How did P. J. feel about going to school? *(excited)*

    3. How did P. J. feel when he thought his beak would grow stronger and his tail feathers would grow longer and more beautiful? *(proud)*

    4. How did P. J.'s older brother, Teddy, feel when P. J. grabbed him and hugged him roughly? *(upset)*

    5. What feelings did the little parrot have when P. J. forgot to use words to get attention and hit him on his back? *(scared/worried)*

    6. When P. J. leaned against Tony, how did Tony feel? *(uncomfortable)*

    7. How did Rosie, Billy, and Susie feel when P. J. squeezed into the block area? *(crowded)*

    8. What feeling did Rosie have when P. J. bumped her, and the tree-home made of blocks fell over? *(frustrated)*

    9. How did Joey feel when P. J. tapped him on the wing and touched his schoolwork? *(annoyed)*

    10. How did Eddie feel when P. J. pushed him on the way to music class? *(angry)*

    11. What feelings did some of the parrots in P. J.'s class have when he screamed out answers and didn't give them a chance to speak? *(shy/embarrassed)*

    12. When students remember the rules and are kind to each other in school, how does everyone feel? *(happy)*

 MAR∗CO PRODUCTS, INC. © 2002 1-800-448-2197

2. **Personal Space Activity:** Have the students do the activities described in the story. Have them pretend to blow up a big balloon, then pretend they are in the center of the balloon. Follow this with a discussion of the concept of *personal space.* Ms. Peggy told the little parrots to stretch out their wings, tail feathers, and beak and turn in a circle. Have the students hold their hands in front of them and turn in a circle. Then discuss personal space. Also have a discussion about a special class signal that students (or the teacher) may use as a reminder if someone forgets the personal space rule.

3. **How Much Personal Space Do We Need?:** Ask the students to line up in a straight line. Explain that when the students walk in a line, they need to respect the personal space of others. They need to keep moving, keep their hands and feet to themselves, and stay together. Give each student a 12" ruler. Explain that the ruler is a good measure of the amount of space to keep between each person. Have the students practice walking and keeping exactly that amount of space between them. Tell the students that they may not hold their rulers up, but that the rulers should be held in their hand beside their bodies. You will say *Stop* as they practice walking. When they hear you say *Stop*, each student will use the ruler to measure the distance between him/herself and the person in front to see if it is the correct distance. Give the line leader a chance to walk in the line so he/she may participate in the measuring activity.

IT'S GOOD NOT TO BE BAD
GRADES 3-5

RESPECT
BEHAVIOR

WRITTEN BY DENA M. HALL

Dena M. Hall is a freelance writer whose daughter's teacher encouraged her to submit this poem for publication. Her poems have also been published by The Iowa Chapter of the National Committee to Prevent Child Abuse, The Foster Family Forum, and Feature Films For Families. She is the mother of four children and resides in Iowa.

IT'S GOOD NOT TO BE BAD

Once upon a time
In a town called Noody Nad
There were many children
Who liked to behave bad.

They picked on their sister
And fought with their brother.
They did not listen to their father,
And they yelled at their mother.

They had many toys to play with,
But still they would not share.
They also like to break things
And didn't even care.

They didn't mind their manners,
And were always much too loud.
All except for one child,
Whose name was I. M. Proud.

He loved his sister and his brother.
He treated his parents with respect.
He always followed the rules they gave him,
Because they made them to protect.

He would try to compromise.
He let others use his things.
He shared because he was thoughtful
And liked the good feeling that sharing brings.

He used his quiet voice at school.
He did not run in stores,
Because he knew you should do that only
When you are out of doors.

People treated him well
And liked to have him around.
They even took him to the carnival,
Where he rode the merry-go-round.

The other children were sad,
And they began to see
Good things would happen to them, too
If they were not so naughty.

They decided they must change their ways
And found it's *good* not to be *bad.*
Then everyone was happy
In the town of Noody Nad.

DISCUSSION QUESTIONS

1. Why do we have rules? *(Rules help us learn the difference between right and wrong. They help make our home, community, and school more pleasant places to be. Accept any other appropriate answers.)*

2. What would it be like if nobody followed the rules? *(There would be no order. People would do whatever they wanted without any consideration for others.)*

3. What would it be like if everybody followed the rules? *(People would be considerate of others, be responsible for their behavior, and be respectful of other people and things.)*

4. What should you do if others do not follow the rules? *(You should not do whatever they are doing. If what they are doing can hurt them or others, you should tell a responsible adult.)*

5. What are some reasons that "It's Good Not To Be Bad"? *(People treat you better, you are happier, and you have good feelings about yourself.)*

6. What are things people do when they behave badly? *(Accept any appropriate answers.)*

7. What are things you can do to act good? *(Accept any appropriate answers.)*

8. How do you behave when you are told to "mind your manners"? *(If you are eating, you use good table manners. If you are with a group of people, you are considerate of others. You behave in the proper way for whatever situation you are in.)*

9. What does it mean to compromise? *(Compromise means to work out a problem so that each person is satisfied with the solution.)*

10. Why did people like to have I. M. Proud around? *(People liked to have him around because he did not run in stores, used his quiet voice at school, was thoughtful, compromised in problem situations, and shared his things with others.)*

FOLLOW-UP ACTIVITIES

1. **It's Good Not To Be Bad:** This game is played like *Simon Says.* Have the leader or a student pretend to be I. M. Proud and act out good and bad behaviors. If the students believe the behavior is good, they should imitate I. M. Proud. If they believe the behavior is bad, they should shake their heads "no" at I. M. Proud. There could be a rule that students who imitate a bad behavior are out of the game. See the suggested list below. For some actions, two people may be required.

2. **Be Good, Be Bad:** This game is played like *Red Light, Green Light.* In this game, the leader or chosen student names good behaviors and the students move forward. As soon as a bad behavior is named, the students must stop. There could be a rule that anyone who doesn't stop when a bad behavior is named is sent back to the starting line. See the suggested list below.

GOOD BEHAVIORS

1. Smiling in a friendly way
2. Reading a book
3. Picking up your things
4. Waiting patiently in line
5. Sharing with your neighbor
6. Drawing a picture
7. Saying *Please*
8. Saying *Thank you*
9. Saying *I'm sorry*
10. Saying *You're welcome*
11. Saying *Excuse me*
12. Using your quiet voice
13. Helping someone get up
14. Letting someone get in line in front of you
15. Raising your hand to get the teacher's attention
16. Opening a door for someone
17. Waving *Hello*
18. Shaking someone's hand
19. Sitting quietly with your hands in your lap
20. Eating politely

BAD BEHAVIORS
1. Cutting in line
2. Poking another person
3. Sticking out your tongue
4. Not sharing
5. Throwing something at someone
6. Tearing up another person's paper
7. Pouting (with arms folded)
8. Making a nasty face
9. Running in the hall
10. Covering your ears with your hands and/or turning your back to people who are talking to you
11. Taking someone's things without asking
12. Using a loud voice in a place where quiet voices should be used
13. Pushing
14. Pulling hair
15. Talking out of turn
16. Hitting someone
17. Jumping on the furniture
18. Slamming the door in someone's face
19. Chewing food with your mouth open
20. Telling a lie

3. **The Manners Game:** Write expressions such as *Excuse me, Please, May I, Thank you, You're welcome, I'm sorry, Hurry up, Get out of the way, Now,* etc. on cards and pin the cards to a bulletin board. Then choose a situation from the following list and ask the students to select the proper response.

1. You accidentally step on someone's toes.
2. You want your mom to get you a drink.
3. You burp.
4. You have just received a present.
5. You break your friend's toy.
6. Someone thanks you for something.
7. Someone is in your way and you want that person to move.
8. You want to borrow a toy.
9. You have hurt someone's feelings.
10. Someone lets you get in front of them in the lunch line.

SPEEDY
GRADES 3-5

TOLERANCE
UNDERSTANDING DIFFERENCES

WRITTEN BY LISA BALL

Lisa Ball is an elementary counselor in Georgia.

Note: This story was originally designed for professionals who work with children diagnosed with Attention Deficit Disorder and for their families. It can be used to explain the role of medication in treating this disorder. It has been modified and can, in this form, also be used in classroom settings to increase tolerant behavior and the understanding of differences.

SPEEDY

Once there was a car named Speedy. Speedy was not like the other cars. He stood out, because he was fast and loud.

(Ask this question only if you are working in an ADD/ADHD situation.) Are *you* ever fast and loud?

Speedy's radio was loud. His horn was loud, and his motor was loud. Speedy also went faster than all the other cars. Being fast caused trouble for Speedy. Sometimes the older cars yelled at Speedy.

(Ask this question only if you are working in an ADD/ADHD situation.) Does that ever happen to you?

Once Speedy even got a ticket for going too fast.

(Ask this question only if you are working in an ADD/ADHD situation.) What happens when *you* get caught going too fast?

Speedy did not understand why everyone was so upset. After all, being fast and loud was fun. Then, while zooming down the road one day, Speedy was not paying attention to a DANGER sign. Before he knew it, he had caused a terrible accident. Speedy was very sad. Everyone seemed to be mad at him. He decided that he would have to slow down and be less noisy.

(Ask this question only if you are working in an ADD/ADHD situation.) Who gets upset when *you* are too loud or too fast?

But no matter how hard he tried, Speedy always ended up going too fast or being too loud.

As he pulled into a gas station one day, Speedy was feeling very discouraged. Charlie, the mechanic, came out to fill Speedy up and noticed that the loud, fast car was crying.

"What's wrong?" Charlie asked.

Speedy looked up at Charlie and said, "No matter how hard I try, I can't be like the other cars. I'm fast and loud, and I always get in trouble."

(Ask this question only if you are working in an ADD/ADHD situation.) Have *you* ever felt like Speedy?

"If you've got a minute, Speedy, I'd like to put you up on the rack and take a look at you," said Charlie.

Speedy nodded his head. Charlie put him up on the rack and took a look at all his parts, but he could find no big problems. Speedy's engine was okay. His tires looked fine. Charlie scratched his head, then said, "I think I can help you. I have some special gas made for fast little cars just like you. Lots of other cars use it."

Speedy's face lit up, "Do you think it could help me?" he asked.

"Well, let's give it a try," said Charlie.

To Speedy's surprise, his motor became less noisy when he started up his car. As he pulled away from the gas station, it became easy not to drive above the speed limit.

Maybe you are like Speedy. If you are, I hope you can learn to cruise slowly and quietly. And Speedy says he will see you on the road.

DISCUSSION QUESTIONS

1. How do you think Speedy got his name? *(He was fast and loud. He went faster than all the other cars and honked his horn and played his radio loudly.)*

2. What do you think the other cars might have said to Speedy? *(Slow down! You're going to hurt someone! Please be quiet! Accept any other appropriate answers.)*

3. Without mentioning any names, just raise your hand if you have you ever heard anyone say these things to another person. *(Wait for the students' response.)*

4. Without mentioning any names, just raise your hand if you think the person to whom these statements are made does not realize why people get upset. *(Wait for the students' response.)*

5. Speedy needed to learn to calm down. What are some things boys and girls can do to calm down when they are upsetting others? *(They can stop what they are doing and think about the other people, take some deep breaths, or count slowly to 10 or higher. Accept any other appropriate answers.)*

6. What can you do to help someone who needs to calm down because he/she is upsetting others? *(Show the person how to calm down by playing a quiet game or telling a responsible adult that the person needs help right away. Accept any other appropriate answers.)*

7. What kind of person tries to help another? *(Someone who is caring, respectful of someone else's needs, tolerant, or understanding. Accept any other appropriate answers. Write these answers on the chalkboard.)*

SUPPLEMENTARY ACTIVITY

Decision-Making: Tell the students you are going to read descriptions of some situations in which a student needs calming down. You will read the description, then give three possible solutions. For each solution, you will point to a place in the classroom. After the students have listened to the three possible solutions, they should move to the place in the classroom designated for the solution they would choose. Once there, they should be able to explain why they made that choice. Emphasize that more than one answer could be correct. After each answer, ask the students to look at the traits listed on the chalkboard from Discussion Question #7 and name the trait their action exemplifies.

1. You are playing a game with a student who is in such a hurry to move her gamepiece that she keeps knocking yours out of the way. Would you suggest playing another game that doesn't require moving gamepieces? Quit the game? Get angry and tell her to "shape up"?

2. You are playing basketball on the playground. One player on your team grabs the ball at every possible chance, even if it is meant for another player on your team. Then, without even thinking what to do, he shoots for a basket. The other team is making all the points. Would you ask that player to leave the game? Stop the game altogether? Suffer through the game and not pick him for your team next time?

3. You have your books neatly stacked on your desk and are working on a math paper. Your classmate jumps out of her seat, walks quickly to the drinking fountain, and walks even faster on the way back. Coming by your desk, she hits your books. They fall all over the floor. As you try to grab your books, your paper sails to the floor and she steps on it. Would you pick up your books and paper and say nothing? Yell at your classmate because of what she had done? Tell the teacher?

4. A classmate wants to answer every question the teacher asks, even if he doesn't know the answer. When the teacher calls on other students, he calls out, "Me, me! Call on me!" Would you let the teacher handle it? Talk with the student outside of class and tell him how the other kids feel? Tell him to "Shut up"?

5. A student is running down the hall, pushing the other kids aside. Would you call a teacher? Just let the kid run on? Try to stop the student?

BEATRICE,
THE BUSY LITTLE BEE
GRADES 1-3

APOLOGIZING
MINDING YOUR OWN BUSINESS

WRITTEN BY WANDA S. COOK

Wanda Cook is an elementary counselor in Texas. She is a contributor to *Special Situations*, published by Mar*co Products.

BEATRICE, THE BUSY LITTLE BEE

"What a lovely morning," thought Beatrice Bee, as she drank from the plump dewdrop that dangled above her hive. Then she breathed in the cool, crisp air and flexed her tiny wings before leaving for the park to gather nectar from the juicy blossoms.

Beatrice loved the beautiful park. She loved zipping from flower to flower to collect the tasty nectar. She loved turning the nectar into thick, delicious honey. Beatrice loved to keep busy. But on this day, Beatrice kept herself busy with things that were not the business of a busy little bee.

It all started that morning in the park, near the bushes with the beautiful white blossoms. Beatrice was busy gathering nectar when she happened to see Suzy Spider. She noticed that Suzy was making something on the opposite side of the bush. Beatrice was curious about what Suzy was making. So she stopped sipping nectar from the sweet-smelling blossoms and flew over to get a closer look.

"Good morning, Suzy," said Beatrice.

"Good morning, Beatrice," replied the spider. "Isn't it a lovely day?"

"A lovely day, indeed," agreed Beatrice.

"It's a lovely day for spinning a web," said Suzy, proudly showing off her web.

"It's a lovely day," said Beatrice, "but *that* is not a lovely web. It's too bad that I'm not a spider. Because if I were, *my* web would be a lovely web."

"Webs are not made to be lovely," said Suzy. "Webs are made to catch food. Bees sip nectar and bees make honey. Spiders make webs. And you are right, Beatrice. You cannot make a web because you are not a spider! You are a bee—a very *busy* little bee. Now I've got work to do, so please go away."

Beatrice made her way back to the other side of the bush and sipped the last bit of sweet nectar from the juicy blossoms. Then she flew away. "What a grumpy little spider," she thought.

Beatrice then zipped over to enjoy the pink blossoms near the center of the garden. As she sipped from the tiny blossoms, she saw Rita Robin. Rita was busy making something in the old oak tree that grew in the middle of the park. Beatrice was curious about what Rita was making, so she stopped sipping nectar and flew over to the oak tree to get a closer look.

"Good morning, Rita," said Beatrice.

"Good morning, Beatrice," replied the robin. "Isn't it a lovely day?"

"A lovely day, indeed," Beatrice agreed.

"It's a lovely day for building a nest," said Rita, proudly showing off her nest.

"It's a lovely day," said Beatrice, "but *that* is not a lovely nest. It's too bad that I'm not a robin. Because if I were, *my* nest would be a lovely nest."

"Nests are not made to be lovely," sobbed Rita. "Nests are homes for baby birds. Bees sip nectar and bees make honey. Robins make nests. And you are right, Beatrice. You cannot make a nest because you are not a robin! You are a bee—a very *busy* little bee. Now I've got work to do, so please go away."

Beatrice returned to the blossoms to sip the last bit of nectar. Then she flew away. "What a weepy little robin," she thought.

The purple blossoms near the back of the garden would be Beatrice's last stop before returning to the hive. As she flew across the pond to reach the delicious blossoms, she noticed that Mother Duck was busy with her ducklings. Beatrice was curious about Mother Duck and her ducklings, so she flew over to get a closer look.

"Good morning, Mother Duck," said Beatrice.

"Good morning, Beatrice," replied the duck. "Isn't it a lovely day?"

"A lovely day, indeed," agreed Beatrice.

"It's a lovely day for walking the ducklings," said Mother Duck, proudly showing off her ducklings.

"It's a lovely day," said Beatrice, "but *those* are not lovely ducklings. It's too bad that I'm not a Mother Duck. Because if I were, *my* ducklings would be lovely ducklings."

"My ducklings *are* lovely," squawked Mother Duck. Hearing their mother squawk, the ducklings squawked, too. "Bees sip nectar and bees make honey. Mother Ducks make ducklings. And you are right, Beatrice. You cannot make a duckling because you are not a duck! You are a bee—a very *busy* little bee. I have ducklings to walk, so please go away," Mother Duck said angrily.

Beatrice made her way to the purple blossoms nestled in the back of the garden. She collected all the nectar she could hold and made a beeline back to the hive. "What an angry Mother Duck," she thought.

In the hive, Beatrice and Becca worked with the other bees to turn the sweet nectar into delicious honey. As they worked, Beatrice told her best friend all about her strange and lovely day. First she told Becca about Suzy Spider, then about Rita Robin. Finally, she told her about Mother Duck.

"Beatrice," Becca scolded after her friend had finished speaking, "you are not a spider, and you cannot make a web. You are not a robin, and you cannot build a nest. You are not a Mother Duck, and you cannot make ducklings. You are a bee, Beatrice, a bee. Bees sip nectar and bees make honey. You have been too busy, Beatrice—much, much too busy, interfering in other people's business when you should have been concerned only with your own."

The other bees who had been listening to Becca and Beatrice agreed with Becca. When Beatrice heard what they had to say she stopped working and buzzed noisily away from the hive. "What fussy little bees," thought Beatrice.

Later that night, Beatrice returned to the hive. She thought about Suzy Spider. She thought about Rita Robin. She thought about Mother Duck. She thought about the ducklings. And she thought about Becca and the other bees.

The next morning, Beatrice returned to the park to collect nectar and to look for Suzy Spider. She found Suzy in the bush, finishing up her web. Beatrice flew over to talk with her.

"Good morning, Suzy," said Beatrice.

Suzy saw Beatrice, but she said nothing. She just continued to spin her web.

"Isn't it a lovely day? A lovely day, indeed," said Beatrice. "In fact, it's a lovely day for spinning a web. And that, Suzy, is a lovely web. It's a lovely web for catching food. You know, bees sip nectar and bees make honey and spiders make webs. I am not a spider. I am a bee, a very *busy* little bee, and I could never make a web as fine as yours. I am very sorry for what I said yesterday. Please forgive me."

Suzy Spider stopped spinning her web. She smiled at Beatrice and said, "Thank you, Beatrice. It is a lovely day—a lovely day, indeed."

Beatrice then sipped nectar from the juicy white blossoms and buzzed off to find Rita Robin. She found Rita in the old oak tree, finishing up her nest. Beatrice flew over to talk with her.

"Good morning, Rita," said Beatrice.

Rita saw Beatrice, but she said nothing. She just continued to build her nest.

"Isn't it a lovely day? A lovely day, indeed," said Beatrice. "In fact, it's a lovely day for building a nest. And that, Rita, is a lovely nest. It's a lovely nest for baby birds. You know, bees sip nectar and bees make honey and robins make nests. I am not a robin. I am a bee, a very *busy* little bee, and I could never make a nest as fine as yours. I am very sorry for what I said yesterday. Please forgive me."

Rita Robin stopped building her nest. She smiled at Beatrice and said, "Thank you, Beatrice. It is a lovely day—a lovely day, indeed."

Beatrice quickly sipped the nectar from the juicy pink blossoms and hurried off to find Mother Duck. She found Mother Duck near the pond, walking her ducklings.

"Good morning, Mother Duck," said Beatrice.

Mother Duck saw Beatrice, but she said nothing. She just continued to walk her ducklings.

"Isn't it a lovely day? A lovely day, indeed," said Beatrice. "In fact, it's a lovely day for walking ducklings. And those are lovely ducklings. You know, bees sip nectar and bees make honey and Mother Ducks make ducklings. I am not a Mother Duck. I am a bee, a very *busy* little bee, and I could never make ducklings as fine as yours. I am very sorry for what I said yesterday. Please forgive me."

Mother Duck stopped walking her ducklings and smiled at Beatrice. The ducklings smiled, too, "Thank you, Beatrice." said Mother Duck. "It is a lovely day—a lovely day, indeed."

An exhausted Beatrice flew back to the hive to look for Becca. She found her working in the hive with the other bees.

"Becca," Beatrice confessed, while buzzing quietly beside her. "I am not a spider and I cannot make a web. Suzy was grumpy because I was too busy and I insulted her. I am not a robin and I cannot build a nest. Rita was weepy because I was too busy and I insulted her. I am not a Mother Duck and I cannot make ducklings. Mother Duck was angry because I was too busy and I insulted her, too. But I am a bee. I sip nectar and I make honey. You were right, Becca, sipping nectar and making honey should be enough business for any little bee. And from now on, this busy little bee will be busy learning not to be too busy with business that is no business of a busy little bee."

Becca stopped working and smiled at Beatrice. The other bees smiled, too. "Beatrice," said Becca, "today is a lovely day—a very lovely day, indeed."

DISCUSSION QUESTIONS

1. What was Beatrice's problem? *(She criticized things others were doing and thought she could have done them better than the others.)*

2. What happened when Beatrice saw Suzy Spider? *(She told Suzy her web was not good and that she could make a better one.)* How did the spider feel after talking with Beatrice? *(She felt grumpy.)*

3. What happened when Beatrice saw Rita Robin? *(She told Rita her nest was not good and that she could build a better one.)* How did the robin feel after talking with Beatrice? *(She felt sad.)*

4. What happened when Beatrice saw Mother Duck and her ducklings? *(She said the ducklings were not lovely, and that if she had ducklings, her ducklings would be lovely.)* How did Mother Duck feel after talking with Beatrice? *(She felt angry.)*

5. When Beatrice went back to the hive, did she realize she had a problem? *(No.)*

6. Who helped Beatrice see that she had a problem? *(Becca helped her.)*

7. How did Beatrice feel after her best friend told her that she had a problem? *(At first, she thought Becca was wrong. But later she realized that Becca was telling the truth.)*

8. Would you want a friend like Becca? Why or why not? *(Accept any appropriate answers.)*

9. What did Beatrice do when she finally realized that *she* was the problem? *(She went back to the spider, robin, and Mother Duck and complimented them and apologized.)*

10. Do you know anyone like Beatrice? *(Allow only yes or no answers.)* Why do you think this person is busy with other people's business? *(Accept any appropriate answers. Do not allow the students to mention any names.)*

SUPPLEMENTARY ACTIVITY

1. **How To Make Friends:** Reproduce *How To Make Friends* (page 159) for each student. Distribute a copy of the activity sheet, a pencil, and crayons to each student. Review the directions and tell the students how much time they have to complete the activity. When the allotted time has elapsed, have the students share their answers with the group.

HOW TO MAKE FRIENDS

Beatrice had to learn how to be friendly to Suzy Spider, Rita Robin, and Mother Duck. Underline the sentences below that are "friendly" sentences.

1. Betty, that is such a pretty sweater.
2. Thomas, your sandwich looks gross!
3. Willie, would you like to eat lunch with me?
4. Daryl, I don't want you on my team because you are not a good player.
5. Diana, you are boring. Don't you ever do anything fun?
6. Sam, you write very nicely.
7. Mandy, would you like to ride bikes after school?
8. Tasha, since your pencil is broken, you may borrow one of mine.
9. Earl, where did you get those awful sneakers?
10. Mikey, would you like to come to my party?

Beatrice apologized to Suzy Spider, Rita Robin, and Mother Duck by going back to each of them and saying something nice. That is only one way to apologize. Pretend you are Beatrice. Think of other ways to apologize. List them below.

1. _____

2. _____

3. _____

On the other side of this paper, draw a picture of yourself and your best friend. Then turn the paper back to this side and explain below why you chose that person as a friend.

_____

_____

_____

URSULA AND THE PINK UMBRELLA
GRADES 3-5

TOLERANCE
PREJUDICE REDUCTION

WRITTEN BY WANDA S. COOK

Wanda Cook, a counselor in Texas, dedicates this story to her two sons, Joseph and John-Michael. She is also a contributor to the book *Special Situations,* published by Mar*co Products.

URSULA AND THE PINK UMBRELLA

A few of the girls in Ursula's class met at Pumpernickel Park each Sunday afternoon to sip peppermint tea and eat tasty crumpets. While enjoying their dainty morsels, they whispered softly and giggled quietly as each eagerly, yet cautiously, shared her most guarded secrets.

Being the new kid in town, Ursula was elated when the friendly girls finally asked her to join them. "Bring an umbrella," they informed her. "An umbrella?" thought Ursula. "How unusual!" But for the people in this small town, it didn't appear to be unusual at all. Ursula had already noticed earlier that *everyone* in her new town always carried an umbrella. She didn't know why, but she wasn't going to question it.

What a glorious Sunday it was! Determined not to be late, Ursula grabbed her pink umbrella and her patent leather purse and hurried to meet her new friends at the silver arch near the park's entrance.

It was at the silver arch that a most spectacular event began to unfold. It was called the *Parade of Umbrellas.* With umbrellas and heads held high, the Pumpernickel Park patrons proudly strolled, single-file, past the shiny silver arch onto a winding and well-adorned walkway which led them to their favorite picnic spot.

What an amazing sight it was! There were all kinds of umbrellas: big ones, little ones, square ones, round ones, shiny ones, dull ones, red ones, green ones, orange ones, purple ones, blue ones with little triangles, silver ones with fat polka dots, fancy ones, and plain ones. But, of all of the umbrellas, only Ursula had a pink one.

Ursula stood with her friends. They were next in line to join the promenade. With umbrellas hoisted and noses in the air, they pranced past the shiny, silver arch onto the well-adorned and winding walkway.

But as Ursula began her walk, a young park attendant grabbed her firmly by the arm. Ursula was startled. "I'm sorry," the park attendant apologized after abruptly stopping her, "but people who carry pink umbrellas are not allowed in Pumpernickel Park."

"No pink umbrellas!" her friends exclaimed in angry disbelief. "How ridiculous! How absurd!"

"No need to fret," said Ursula gently, trying to calm her friends. "I'll simply return the pink umbrella, exchange it for another, and join you here later."

So Ursula left the park and returned to *Fancy Frances Boutique,* where she had shopped the day before. She had gone into the shop because of the banana- and cream-colored umbrella that was attractively displayed in the store window. The owner, who didn't seem too friendly, refused to sell Ursula the elegant banana- and cream-colored umbrella and *insisted* that she purchase the pale pink one instead. When that happened, Ursula left the boutique without the umbrella that she wanted. She felt unhappy, annoyed, and very confused.

"But that was yesterday," she thought optimistically as she entered the boutique with its beautiful beveled glass doors. "Today will be different." Once she was inside, Ursula flashed the owner a warm smile before politely explaining her unfortunate predicament. After listening to her story, the unfriendly owner looked indifferently into Ursula's pleading eyes. Then she folded her arms. Speaking in a slow, humiliating manner, she informed Ursula that under no circumstances would the boutique *ever* consider making *any* exchanges for people who carry pink umbrellas.

Ursula's warm smile vanished. Things were no different today than they had been the day before. Once again, she left the boutique without her banana- and cream-colored umbrella, feeling unhappy, annoyed, and very confused. "It's not that important," she said to herself, refusing to feel defeated.

Ursula decided to forget her troubles by treating herself to a luscious strawberry sundae at the famed *2000 Flavors Ice Cream Parlor* next to the boutique. She entered the parlor, grabbed a number, and patiently waited her turn. "Number 7," yelled the young cashier. Ursula, anticipating the taste of her thick, rich, creamy dessert, rushed to the counter to place her order. But the young cashier, who was chewing ferociously on a big wad of green gum, stopped short and gave her a most puzzling look. After slowly and forcefully shifting his gum to his lower left cheek, he asked if she had read the small sign in the store window. "I'm sorry," he said as he struggled to speak, "but we don't serve people who carry pink umbrellas."

As the words poured out of his mouth his gum fell onto the counter. Ursula felt defeated. She didn't think she was going to like her new town.

By Monday morning, all was forgotten and Ursula eagerly anticipated the events of a new school week. Riding the school bus for the first time seemed to add a sense of excitement to an ordinary school morning. The other students didn't appear to share Ursula's early morning enthusiasm. They waited in silence until the rickety old school bus appeared, its blinking neon lights shattering the stillness and thickness of the early foggy morning.

Ursula stepped onto the bus. She was pleased to see other children who carried pink umbrellas, but thought it odd that they all sat on the rear right side of the bus. She decided to take the first seat on the left side, next to a little girl who immediately flashed her a friendly smile and who carried a vibrant and elegant banana- and cream-colored umbrella.

The two chatted as they waited for the other students to find seats. They chatted and waited. They waited and chatted—completely unaware of the bus driver's quiet protest. Then William Wayne Franklin's long, pointy finger tapped Ursula's narrow shoulder. "Please," he said, "you'll make us all late. She won't move the bus until you sit on the rear right side of the bus with the other children who carry pink umbrellas." Ursula glanced up and saw the bus driver's disapproving look. "It's time to talk with my parents about our strange new town," Ursula silently declared as she moved slowly to the rear and sat on the right side of the rickety old school bus.

Shocked and disturbed, Ursula's parents decided that every concerned citizen of the town needed to hear Ursula's unbelievable story. Her father called the mayor. The mayor called a meeting. The mayor also called his assistant, Molly. Molly called the young park attendant, the unfriendly boutique owner, the gum-chewing cashier, and the scowling bus driver. Ursula's mother called everyone else, including all the people who carried pink umbrellas.

The meeting was scheduled for Saturday at the town square, next to Mr. Gioletti's Gourmet Bakery. That was where Ursula's friends purchased their tasty Sunday crumpets.

On the day of the meeting, the town square was transformed into a colorful sea of splendid umbrellas with rows and rows of pink umbrellas. Ursula stood with her parents, the mayor, the police chief, the fire marshal, and several ladies who carried fancy banana- and cream-colored umbrellas. All of her new friends were there, and so was the little girl with the friendly smile from the school bus. She stood near William Wayne Franklin.

The town citizens wailed in disbelief when they heard Ursula's distressing story.

"It wasn't my fault," protested the young park attendant, as he rose in his defense. "The boutique owner told me that *all* people who carry pink umbrellas were *stubborn* and *impolite*. I didn't want that kind of trouble at the park, so I decided not to let them in."

"And *he* told *me*," admitted the gum-chewing cashier, pointing to the young park attendant. "I decided not to serve people who carry pink umbrellas because I was afraid that stubborn, impolite, *ill-mannered troublemakers* would frighten away the other customers."

"And *he* warned *me* about people who carry pink umbrellas," declared the scowling bus driver, pointing to the gum-chewing cashier. "I decided that all stubborn, impolite, ill-mannered, *obnoxious* troublemakers should sit on the rear right side of the school bus so the other students would feel safe."

The unfriendly boutique owner had no defense.

After a long and unsettling silence, the mayor began to speak. "People who carry pink umbrellas are as kind and gentle as most of the citizens of our honorable community," he said. "If citizens have been treated unfairly, it is their right to protest. And while they are protesting, they should remain immovable. That is neither stubborn nor impolite. It is neither ill-mannered nor obnoxious. It is noble. If there is anyone in this fine and upstanding town who should be labeled *stubborn, impolite, ill-mannered, and obnoxious trouble makers,*" the mayor scolded as he addressed the accused, "it is each of you! I HEREBY DECREE From This Day Forward: That citizens of this fine town have the right to carry the umbrellas of their choice."

"And," the mayor continued, "that citizens of this fine town have the right to make an exchange if the above privilege has in any way been denied. And, finally, that citizens of this honorable town have the right to visit the park or ice cream parlor regardless of the size, shape, or color of their umbrellas. The unfair treatment of people who carry pink umbrellas will exist no more."

The crown roared a warm and hearty cheer! As did the police chief, the fire marshal, the ladies who carried the fancy banana- and cream-colored umbrellas, Ursula's new friends, the little girl from the school bus, and William Wayne Franklin.

The *Parade of Umbrellas* the following Sunday was peculiar, yet it was the most extraordinary one the townspeople had ever seen! It seemed that those who had once carried big umbrellas now carried small ones. Others who had once carried small umbrellas, now carried square ones. Some who had carried square umbrellas now carried round ones. Round umbrellas had been exchanged for shiny ones, shiny ones for dull ones, dull ones for red ones, red ones for green ones, green ones for orange ones, orange ones for blue ones with triangles, blue ones with triangles for silver ones with fat polka dots, silver ones with fat polka dots for fancy ones, and fancy ones for plain ones. *But it seemed that most umbrellas had been exchanged for pink umbrellas!*

With umbrellas and heads held high *all* Pumpernickel Park patrons strolled even more proudly than before past the shiny, silver arch onto the well-adorned and winding walkway.

"I think I am going to like my new town," thought Ursula proudly, as she lead the promenade, carrying her new elegant and vibrant banana- and cream-colored umbrella.

DISCUSSION QUESTIONS

1. What was so unusual about Ursula's new town? *(People discriminated against people with pink umbrellas.)*

2. Describe the different types of umbrellas in the parade at Pumpernickel Park. *(There were big ones, little ones, square ones, round ones, shiny ones, dull ones, red ones, green ones, orange ones, purple ones, blue ones with little triangles, silver ones with fat polka dots, fancy ones, and plain ones.)*

3. Describe Ursula's first umbrella. *(It was pink.)*

4. What happened when Ursula tried to join the promenade with her friends? *(She was told she couldn't participate, because she was carrying a pink umbrella.)*

5. Why do you think Ursula carried a pink umbrella? *(It was what the boutique owner talked her into buying.)* Which umbrella did she really want? *(She wanted a banana- and cream-colored one.)*

6. How were people with pink umbrellas treated differently from people who carried other umbrellas? *(They had to sit on certain seats on the bus, weren't served in the ice cream parlor, couldn't participate in the promenade, and were not allowed to exchange purchases they had made.)*

7. Did all the town's people have the freedom to purchase the umbrella of their choice? *(No.)*

8. Have you ever been treated meanly because others saw you as being different? *(Accept any appropriate answers.)* Discuss this concept with the students.

9. Whom did Ursula go to for help? *(She went to her parents.)*

10. Who was responsible for spreading rumors about people who carried pink umbrellas? *(The boutique owner started the rumors.)*

11. How did the story end? *(The mayor forbade anyone from discriminating against any citizen.)*

FOLLOW-UP ACTIVITIES

1. **Likenesses And Differences:** Some people are alike and some are different. All people deserve respect. Have the students discuss how they are alike and different from the other students in the class. If desired, distribute art paper and have the students draw this activity.

2. **Feeling Words:** All people have feelings. Have the students name some feelings that everyone has. Write those *feeling words* on the chalkboard.

3. **Name-Calling:** It hurts when mean things are said to someone who is different. Discuss whether this has ever happened to any of the students and how it felt.

4. **Likenesses And Differences:** Reproduce *Likenesses And Differences* (page 171) for each student. Distribute the activity sheet and a pencil to each student. Tell the students to look for both the likenesses and differences between themselves and the person pictured and to write their answers on the lines below each picture. When everyone has finished the activity, discuss the students' answers.

5. **Different Foods, Music, Dancing, And Dressing:** Reproduce *Different Foods, Music, Dancing, And Ways Of Dressing* (page 172) for each student. Distribute the activity sheet and a pencil to each student. Tell the students that people enjoy all different kinds of food, music, dancing, and ways of dressing. Have the students name their favorite type of music and music that others may enjoy listening or dancing to. Then have them do the same with different foods and ways of dressing. When the students have completed the activity sheet, have them share their answers with the group.

6. **Problem-Solving:** Reproduce *Situations: Which Is The Best Solution?* (page 173) for each student. Distribute the activity sheet and a pencil to each student. Have the students read each description and circle the best solution.

Name _____

LIKENESSES AND DIFFERENCES

Directions: Below are six pictures. Look at each one and describe how each is different from or like you. It is okay to be both alike and different from a picture.

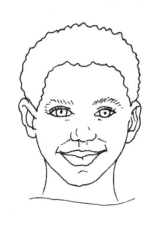

ALIKE_____
_____
_____

DIFFERENT _____
_____
_____

ALIKE_____
_____
_____

DIFFERENT _____
_____
_____

ALIKE_____
_____
_____

DIFFERENT _____
_____
_____

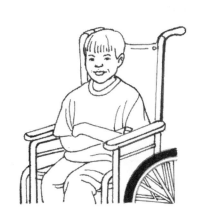

ALIKE_____
_____
_____

DIFFERENT _____
_____
_____

ALIKE_____
_____
_____

DIFFERENT _____
_____
_____

ALIKE_____
_____
_____

DIFFERENT _____
_____
_____

DIFFERENT FOODS, MUSIC, DANCING, AND WAYS OF DRESSING

Name your favorite type of music.

_____

What other kinds of music might others enjoy listening or dancing to?

_____

_____

_____

Moy-Chung loves eating Mexican food. Name other kinds of food that people enjoy.

_____

_____

_____

Have you ever dressed like someone from a different country?

_____

If so, how did you dress? Why did you dress that way?

_____

_____

_____

_____

_____

In the space below, draw a picture of your favorite way to dress.

SITUATIONS: WHICH IS THE BEST SOLUTION?

Directions: Read each situation. Then circle the solution which you believe to be best.

1. Ming Li brings an unusual sandwich for lunch. It looks and smells different from the other students' sandwiches. Which is the best solution?

   a. Hold your nose and say *yuk!*
   b. Politely ask her about her sandwich.
   c. Move to another table.
   d. None of the above.

2. Muhan's family is very different from those of the other students in her class. Her family celebrates different holidays and she dresses differently from the other students. Which is the best solution?

   a. Ask the other students not to associate with Muhan because she is different.
   b. Tell Muhan to move to a school where there are other students like her.
   c. Try to learn more about Muhan's family and her culture.
   d. None of the above.

3. Roberto speaks two different languages. He speaks English in school and he speaks Spanish at home. He would love to speak both of his languages at school, but he is afraid that others may tease him. Which is the best solution?

   a. He could not speak at all during school.
   b. He could offer to teach his English-speaking friends to speak Spanish.
   c. He could speak only English at school.
   d. None of the above.

4. Ashley wants to play a circle game with the other students. Her wheelchair won't fit neatly into the circle. Which is the best solution?

   a. Tell her to play with her own kind.
   b. Ignore her.
   c. Tell her she can play only if she gets out of her wheelchair to do so.
   d. None of the above.

TAKE GOOD CARE OF YOUR WET PET, AND OF EACH OTHER, TOO!
GRADES 1-3

CARING
KINDNESS
RESPONSIBILITY

WRITTEN BY BETSY DAVIDSON

Betsy Davidson lives in New Mexico and dedicates this story to all the living creatures on this earth. She is also the author of *Twyla Tulip And Her Talking Toes*, published by Mar*co Products.

 MAR*CO PRODUCTS, INC. © 2002 1-800-448-2197

TAKE GOOD CARE OF YOUR WET PET, AND OF EACH OTHER, TOO!

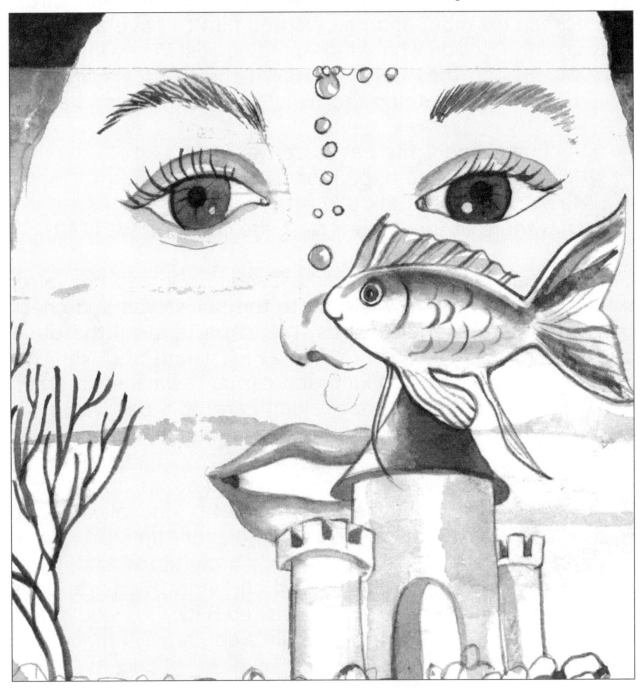

Suction was a pretty fish.
A pretty fish was he.
Suction had just one wish:
To find a loving family.

Gus was 10 years old. He didn't have any sisters or brothers. Gus really wanted a pet. But Gus lived in an apartment where no one was allowed to have cats or dogs or even birds. Sometimes his mom and dad wanted him to have a pet, but they couldn't decide what kind would be best. They loved Gus very much, and they believed that if they kept trying, they would think of something that would make their son happy.

> Suction thought the pet store was okay,
> But he hoped and hoped for something better.
> He swam in that tank day after day,
> Knowing that in a bigger tank, he could be WETTER!

Gus had made many nice friends at school. Sometimes, after school, some of them would go to the pet stores and check out the puppies, kittens, birds, hamsters, and all the other critters. Most of Gus' friends had at least one pet. Not only were Gus and his friends kind and caring toward each other, but each of them knew that taking care of a pet was a big responsibility that required kindness, patience, and love.

Gus' one friend, Billy, had a dog. Billy walked his dog at least three times a day, and he made sure his dog always had water. He fed his dog at the same time every day. Billy's dog was very loyal and well-behaved. Billy understood that it was right to be kind and caring toward all living things, and his dog was a living thing. When Gus visited Billy, Gus would help Billy with his dog. Helping with Billy's dog always made Gus feel good, too.

> Suction had heard stories about getting a bad owner,
> Stories so scary they made his fins palpitate.
> He knew if that happened, he could be a goner.
> So he tried not to think it could be his fate.

One day, a group of boys walked into Suction's pet store. They made Suction nervous. He didn't like these boys. They were loud, and they said things that didn't sound very nice. They even said things about each other that weren't very nice.

The boys walked over to the tank where Suction was swimming. One of the boys, whose name was Bobby, liked the way Suction looked. Bobby called the owner of the store and, in what seemed like seconds, bought Suction. He took Suction home and threw him in a bowl that he had in his room. The bowl was dirty, and Suction had bad feelings right away. Oddly enough, Bobby was in Gus' class, but they weren't close friends.

Bobby fed Suction that first day. But five more days passed, and Suction didn't get any more food. Suction was getting very skinny. Each day, he grew more and more sad.

> Suction did not know what to do.
> He didn't have much of a choice.
> He wanted to scream until he turned blue,
> But suction did not have a voice!

When Bobby's mom walked into his room and saw Suction, she felt very sad. She knew Bobby wasn't really a bad boy, but she also knew he wasn't taking responsibility for his new pet. He wasn't showing much consideration toward his parents if he believed he could shift the responsibility of taking care of Suction to them. Mother decided to give Bobby a few more days before taking action. But Bobby did not change. When Mother saw how skinny Suction was getting, she went to Dad. After talking it over, they both decided not to let Suction suffer any longer.

Mother scooped Suction up, put him in some water, and took him back to the store where Bobby had purchased him. When Bobby came home, he was told that Suction was gone and that he would not be allowed to have any pets until he learned caring and responsibility toward other living creatures.

Bobby really felt bad that he hadn't taken better care of Suction. When he had first seen Suction, his intentions had been good. But he was afraid his friends would make fun of him if they knew he was being kind and loving toward this little fish. Now he was starting to realize that it pretty much didn't matter what other people thought. What really mattered was what made you feel good inside. And Bobby did not feel good inside.

> Suction was put into another tank
> Where the water was kind of clouded.
> He had gotten so skinny, he almost sank
> In this tank that was terribly crowded.

One rainy Saturday, when Gus was feeling kind of sad and lonely, he walked into a pet store he had never been in before. He was alone. He looked at the birds and the puppies and all the other critters. The more he looked, the worse he felt, because he couldn't have one. Then he looked to the back of the store and saw a bunch of fish tanks loaded with fish and snails and even lizards and frogs. He looked into one tank and then another. He was hoping there just might be something he would be able to take home.

Then he saw Suction. Even though Suction was so skinny, Gus saw how beautiful the little fish was. He wanted to give a good home to this pretty fish. Gus actually felt like Suction was looking right at him. He knew he could not buy the fish without his parents' permission, so he ran all the way home.

Suction smiled broadly when Gus came by.
He liked him right away.
But he certainly didn't understand why
Gus didn't want to stay.

When Gus got home, he was so excited that he couldn't stop talking about the pretty little fish that seemed to look right up at him. It made his mom and dad happy to see Gus so happy. Of course, a fish would be okay in an apartment. So off the three of them went to the pet store.

Gus walked quickly over to the tank that held Suction. Suction swam up to the front of the tank and seemed to be looking right at Gus again. Gus put a great big smile on his face and showed his parents the fish that had made him so excited.

Gus' parents told him that taking care of this little fish was a big responsibility. Gus said he knew that and promised he would love this little fish and always take care of him. His parents bought a special tank and all the equipment and food they needed for the little fish. With packages under their arms and Suction in a plastic bag, Gus, his mom, and his dad went home. Then they set up the tank and put Suction into it.

Suction was happy with so much room,
And water that wasn't mucky.
He didn't feel doom and gloom.
In fact, he now felt lucky!

Gus' class had a school project. Everyone was to bring something he or she was proud of. Gus brought Suction and showed a picture of how Suction looked when he first got him and what he looked like now. One look at Suction's picture, and everyone could see that Suction was one beautiful fish.

Bobby, who we remember was in Gus' class, recognized Suction. Although he felt really bad about how he had treated Suction, he now felt really happy that Suction was in such good hands. Bobby started talking with Gus about Suction. As they talked, Bobby began to realize how nice Gus was. He saw that Gus was just as caring toward him as he was toward Suction. He wondered why he hadn't noticed sooner what a great friend Gus could be.

The next day, Bobby brought to school a model airplane that he had built. He explained to Gus just how he had done it. One thing led to another, and soon the boys became good friends.

Gus taught Bobby how great it can be when you care for a pet. Bobby learned about not only showing caring and responsibility toward a pet, but also toward other people. Bobby taught Gus how to build model airplanes. Yes, they both learned from each other. Bobby even felt that he was ready for a pet of his own. But he also knew that for a while, he would have to be satisfied to visit Suction.

> Suction swam and swam and swam,
> Fins wiggling and a wide grin upon his face,
> For the very first, time he wasn't crammed!
> He was in a roomy, healthy, loving, place!

Gus took such good care of Suction that the fish grew bigger and more beautiful each day. Suction always had a clean tank and just enough food to keep him happy. Bobby visited Gus and Suction often. Bobby was happy to have Gus for a friend. Gus was happy to have Bobby for a friend. Bobby and Gus were happy for Suction. Gus' parents were happy for Gus. Bobby's parents were happy for Bobby. And as for Suction, well, he was just happy!

DISCUSSION QUESTIONS

1. Why do you think Gus wanted a pet? *(He wanted something to love and care for. Accept any other appropriate answers.)*

2. Why did Gus have many nice friends at school? *(Gus had many nice friends at school because Gus was kind and caring toward others.)*

3. Why was Billy's dog loyal and well-behaved? *(Billy's dog was loyal and well-behaved because the animal was shown love and was well-cared for.)*

4. What should Bobby have done before he took Suction home? *(He should have asked for permission from his parents and made sure he had a clean place for the fish.)*

5. What did Bobby do to Suction that wasn't very nice? *(He put him in a dirty bowl, didn't feed him regularly, and ignored him.)*

6. What did Gus do that was the right way to go about buying a pet? *(He asked permission from his parents.)*

7. Why did Gus' parents tell him that taking care of this little fish was a big responsibility? *(They wanted to make sure Gus would take care of Suction properly and wanted to teach Gus responsibility.)*

8. Why was Bobby able to become friends with Gus and Suction? *(Bobby was able to become friends with Gus and Suction because he started to become a caring and responsible individual.)*

9. What made Suction, Gus' parents, Bobby's parents, Gus, and Bobby happy? *(Suction was being loved and taken care of by a good owner. Gus' parents were happy that Gus took responsibility. Bobby's parents were happy that he learned caring and responsibility from a friend. Gus and Bobby were happy seeing Suction happy and making each other happy.)*

FOLLOW-UP ACTIVITIES

1. **Animal Responsibility:** Distribute art paper and crayons or markers to each student. Tell the students to divide their paper into three sections. Label the sections *apartment, house, farm*. In each section, have the students draw pictures or write the names of animals that could be pets in each situation. When all the students have finished, have them tell what responsibilities they would have if any of these animals were their pets. Then have the students turn their paper over and, in large letters, write the word *Responsibility*. Explain that *responsibility* is a character trait students would need if they were to have a pet.

2. **Fish:** Reproduce the picture of the fish (page 183) for each student. Distribute a copy of the fish activity, scissors, crayons or markers, and a pencil to each student. Tell the students to complete the sentence written on the fish, cut it out, and color it any way they desire. When all the students have finished coloring the fish, attach the fish to a bulletin board. Or attach the fish to the wall, as if they are swimming around the room.

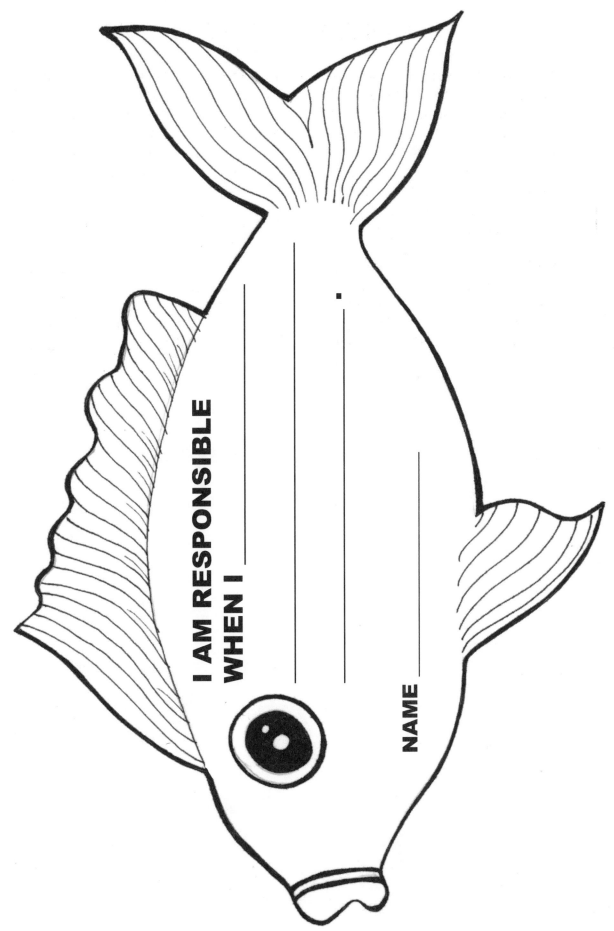

I AM RESPONSIBLE WHEN I

NAME

BAKER WAS A GOOD DOG, OR WAS HE?
GRADES 3-5

CARING
LOVE

WRITTEN BY ANITA DEYOUNG

Anita DeYoung is a former teacher from Pennsylvania.

BAKER WAS A GOOD DOG,
OR WAS HE?

Baker was a good dog, or at least *he* thought he was. It was just that he had a lot of energy and that energy landed him in trouble. Why this happened, he didn't know. Because he certainly didn't plan to get into trouble.

Baker lived with Mona and Dan. They would play with him and take him for walks. Baker would do almost anything to make them happy, and Baker felt loved. At bedtime, Baker had a special kennel where he had a nice soft towel to lie on. There wasn't much room in the kennel, but it was good enough for sleeping. When morning came, Baker would go outside for a little while and then have to come inside for the dreaded "bad time."

The bad time was when Mona and Dan left. They left each morning, and Baker did not like being left alone. There he was, penned up in the kitchen with nothing to do but sit on the floor in front of the stove, walk around the chair, sit in front of the sink, or walk around the table. It made no sense to Baker that at this time, he wasn't allowed to go upstairs or visit the other rooms. This was definitely not fun. All he could think of was how much he would like to run and chase something. Then he had a little doggie thought, "Wouldn't it be neat if I could jump as high as the gate?"

What started out as a little thought turned into a challenge. First, Baker warmed up with little hops. Then he decided to practice some high leaps. Those leaps were difficult, because if he didn't do them right, Baker would slip on the floor. All that jumping made Baker tired and thirsty, so he drank his water and took a nap. When he woke up, he was really full of energy and ready to try again. All the practice he had had in the morning must have been good for his style, because after a few warmups, he was up and over the gate and into the dining room. He could hardly wait to have Mona and Dan see what he had accomplished! They were sure to be proud of him!

Being free was great. There were things to sniff, things to jump on, things to roll on, things to pull on, and things to chew. Life didn't get any better than this. Baker whirled around from room to room, finding more and more exciting things to do. All this excitement and the drinks of water he had had in the morning caused a nasty thing to happen on the bedroom rug! Baker couldn't believe it! He had never done anything like that before. What would Mona and Dan think? He decided he had better jump up on the bed and think it over while he rested.

Click! Click! Click! The sound of Mona's footsteps coming up the stairs woke Baker. He didn't know what to do. He always greeted her in the kitchen. But he knew she would be happy to see him and to learn all about the exciting day he had had.

As Mona walked into the bedroom, she was saying really, really loud things. Baker didn't realize she was talking to him until he saw her face. She was very, very angry! Her loud words were for him, and they were not nice. Baker jumped down off the bed and quickly ran under it. As he turned around, he could see Mona's face peering under the bedspread. She was looking right at him. Baker thought he'd better get out of there. And since he had never been in a situation like this, all he could think to do was run. As he scrambled out from under the bed, the little rug went flying. Baker whirled around the corner and bolted down the stairs. He thought he would be safe if he went to the kitchen and sat on his little mat. But as he was running through the dining room, he heard Dan come in the door. At the same time, he heard a big "thud" from upstairs. Mona screamed, and Dan called to her. Dan took the gate away and ran upstairs, still calling to Mona. Baker thought it would be a good thing if he just stayed in the kitchen and waited for them to come down to see him.

When Mona opened Baker's kennel door to let him outside the next morning she didn't talk to him or pet him. He wasn't sure what that meant, but it didn't make him feel good. He asked himself, "Doesn't she care about me any more?" When Mona was ready to leave, she didn't put the gate up. Instead she called Baker and pointed to his kennel! "She must be confused," Baker thought. "It isn't bedtime. I'm not tired. I'm full of pep and ready to play. She can't mean for me to spend the 'bad time' in the kennel." The next thing he knew, Baker was in the kennel, the door had snapped shut, and Mona had left through the kitchen door.

The day was long. Baker's little puppy brain couldn't understand how he had gotten in such trouble. He wanted to move around, but in his kennel he could only sit or lie down. He chewed on his soft towel until he had a pile of pieces. Then he took a nap. Time passed slowly until Mona came home.

It was good to see her. Baker started wagging his tail and hopping with excitement. Mona opened the wire door and said loud words again! Baker couldn't believe his ears. "What had gone wrong? Why did she sound so mad?" he asked himself. As Mona opened the kitchen door for him to go outside, she made stomping sounds with her feet. Once outside, Baker heard the kitchen door slam. He was alone. Mona didn't come out with him. No play time, no walk ... What had he done?

Discussion Opportunity: Stop the story and ask the students the following questions:
1. Why was Baker in trouble again? *(He chewed the towel to pieces.)*
2. Why do you think he was doing these things? *(He was lonely. Accept any other appropriate answers.)*

When Dan came home, he wasn't any happier than Mona to see Baker. There were no sticks thrown, no running fast and returning them, and no walk with the snaky thing on his collar. Baker had waited all day and it wasn't going to happen. Baker was sad and lonely. Instead of sitting in someone's lap, he was told to stay on the floor.

Baker was not sure how long he could spend days and nights in his kennel and still be a happy dog. Whenever Dan and Mona went anywhere, Baker was put in his kennel. He had to stay there all the time they were gone. Life was getting very dull, and the worst part was that Baker still had a lot of energy and wanted to run around and play. He didn't think that Dan and Mona loved him any more or that they even wanted him to be their dog. Baker wasn't sure what he could do, but he did know that he didn't want to live like that.

Then Baker found something to do to pass the time he spent in the kennel. He discovered that he had a good singing voice, and he began to practice every day. At least this was something he could do that wouldn't take up much space or get him in trouble. He developed a nice group of tunes that had some howls, yaps, barks, yips, and woofs in them. He thought that if his singing could take up enough of his time, he would be all right after all.

Then, one evening when Dan and Mona arrived home, they had a stranger with them. The stranger seemed unhappy, and when they all were in the kitchen, the stranger pointed to

Baker in his little kennel and said some loud things. Shortly after that, the stranger left. Mona and Dan sat down at the table and looked at each other. Then they looked at Baker. They didn't look happy, and they kept shaking their heads from side to side. When they let Baker out into the back yard, he was all alone again. "Maybe if I take a little stroll by myself, I'll get rid of some of my energy," thought Baker, "and maybe then I'll come home a better dog."

Discussion Opportunity: Stop the story and ask the students the following questions:
1. What had Baker spent the day doing? *(He had been howling, but he thought he was singing)* Why? *(He was lonely and confined to the kennel.)*
2. Who was the stranger? *(The stranger was Mona and Dan's neighbor.)*
3. What did the stranger say to Mona and Dan? *(He told them that their dog had been howling all day.)*
4. Why do you think Baker went for a stroll? *(He was sad and confused. He thought that if he used up some of his energy, he might come home a better dog.)*

After following many twists and turns, going around many bends, and crossing lots of paths, Baker was very confused. He didn't know his way home, and he wasn't sure what to do about it. He walked and walked, but he couldn't find the smells that he knew marked the way back to his house. He was also very tired. "It's best," he thought, "if I take a little nap and then work on getting back home."

Baker woke up in the arms of a man wearing a dark suit and cap. Baker did not know what would happen next, but the man was looking at the tags hanging from Baker's collar. Baker was getting scared. Maybe the walk had been a bad idea. He wondered if he would ever see Mona and Dan again. And if he did, would *they* want to see *him*?

Baker didn't know it, but that evening he was a lucky, lucky dog! The man in the dark suit was a police officer. Not just any police officer, but a canine officer. He had a special interest in dogs, and he knew a lot about them. One of the things he knew about was why Baker was in trouble so much. He helped Dan and Mona realize that Baker had a lot of energy and needed a lot of exercise and special attention.

Baker was very tired when he arrived home. He was so happy to see his little kennel! It was just the right size and it felt very safe and cozy. He was happy to have a fluffy new towel to lay on. Exhausted, he rolled up in a ball and went right to sleep.

When Dan and Mona came downstairs the next morning, Dan had the long snaky thing in his hand. He and Baker went for a fast, fun walk. When it was time for Mona and Dan to leave, Baker didn't have to stay in his kennel for the day. He was allowed to be in the kitchen again. He also found some new toys that he could play with during the day. Baker was happy. He chewed on a big rawhide bone and played with a squeaky toy instead of singing. He tried to keep busy all day and wait patiently for the special click of Mona's shoes. He loved that sound. When Mona arrived home, she was smiling. She said nice things to Baker in the voice that he liked so much. He was so happy when she took him outside and brought the ball along! He knew that he would get to chase it and run really, really fast. That would make them both happy, because ... Baker was a good dog!

DISCUSSION QUESTIONS

1. Baker felt lonely and confused because he did not understand why Mona and Dan were acting different than usual. Has this ever happened to you? *(Accept any appropriate answers.)* What did you do? *(Accept any appropriate answers.)*

2. Do you think it's hard to stay out of trouble when you feel bored, lonely, or have lots of energy to burn? Why? *(Accept any appropriate answers.)*

3. Baker wanted Mona and Dan's attention. What kinds of things do you do to get your parents' attention? *(Accept any appropriate answers.)*

4. How did you know that Mona and Dan really loved and cared for Baker? *(They took him for walks and played with him.)*

5. How do you know that your parents love and care for you? *(Accept any appropriate answers.)*

SUPPLEMENTARY ACTIVITY

1. **Caring:** Reproduce *Caring* (page 193) for each student. Distribute a copy of the activity sheet and a pencil to each student. When everyone has completed the activity sheet, have the students share their work with the group. Then ask several students complete the following sentence stem:

    I act in a caring way when I _____ .

CARING

Three people who care for me are:

1. _____

2. _____

3. _____

I know these people care for me because they _____

_____ .

Three people I care for are:

1. _____

2. _____

3. _____

These people know I care for them because I _____

_____ .

Draw a face that
shows how you
feel when people act
in a caring way toward you.

THE LAND OF OGDEN
GRADES 3-5

RESPECT
COOPERATION
TOLERANCE

WRITTEN BY WANDA S. COOK

Wanda Cook is an elementary counselor in Texas. She is a contributor to *Special Situations*, published by Mar*co Products.

 MAR*CO PRODUCTS, INC. © 2002 1-800-448-2197

THE LAND OF OGDEN

The Land of Ogden was filled with peaceful streams, sun-kissed mountains, and thick clusters of trees that formed a soft emerald blanket around the country's fertile valleys.

Dragons roamed freely in this vast and mythical land. And from all appearances, Ogden was a perfectly peaceful kingdom. But things in this great land were not as they seemed.

In years past, the dragons in Ogden had been very friendly. For many years, they had lived together happily in their beautiful kingdom. Then one day, without any explanation, the dragons announced to the king that they wished to live in separate colonies. And so it happened that:

> Dragons who gave the king fire and those who gathered the king's stones settled in the Northern regions.

> Those who hunted and farmed the land settled in the Eastern regions.

> The king's potters and his waterbearers settled in the Southern regions.

> And his bakers and chariotmakers settled in the Western regions.

Although the dragons lived in separate colonies, they agreed to work hard and be neighborly for the sake of King Benjamin, the kind and noble ruler of the land. But try as they might, the dragons found themselves engaged in bitter quarrels almost every day. They quarreled because each colony believed that it had the most important job in the kingdom. Each colony believed that because its job was such an important job, their colony was far superior to any of the other colonies of Ogden dragons.

This attitude confused King Benjamin. He could not understand the dragons' behavior, especially since he was such a generous man. Each day, after the king had acquired his royal portion, the Ogden dragons were privileged to partake of the king's water, his fire, his stones, his chariots, his spoils from the hunt, his pottery, the riches of his farm land, and his bread. "Having all of these privileges should make them happy," the king thought.

He was also saddened because he knew the dangers of being discontent. He often met with the dragons and told them of the dangers of living in a kingdom that was divided against itself and one in which no one had respect for others. He would often warn, "Where there is no respect, there is no honor." But the colonies, though they regarded the king highly, had a great need to feel superior.

Soon there was so much feuding in the Land of Ogden that the dragons could not complete their daily chores. There were days when the dragons produced so little that there was hardly enough left of the king's royal portion for them to share among themselves. This made the quarreling worse. Eventually, their quarreling caused such a rift in the kingdom that there were days when even the king did not receive his royal portion.

News of the feuding Ogden dragons quickly spread throughout all the land and into the neighboring Kingdom of Id. The wicked ruler of Id, King Jonus, had always envied the kind and generous King Benjamin. His envy had turned to hate, and with the dragons in such a state of discontent, King Jonus decided that this was the perfect time to seize King Benjamin's land of peaceful streams and sun-kissed mountains and claim it as his own.

Early the next morning, while the dragons slept, the wicked king and his army invaded the Land of Ogden and ...

They captured King Benjamin's fire dragons and his stone dragons.

They captured King Benjamin's farmer dragons and his hunter dragons.

They captured King Benjamin's potter dragons, water bearer dragons, baker dragons, and chariotmaker dragons.

They even captured King Benjamin and forced him to live as a prisoner in his own palace.

Then the wicked king ordered that the captured dragons be taken to the Land of Id and thrown into a cold, dark cave. Though they were surprised and angered by King Jonus' early-morning invasion, the feuding Ogden dragons were even more outraged because they were now forced to live in the same quarters.

They sat silently, shivering in the darkness, too stubborn to speak, too stubborn to make peace. Days passed and their feelings of arrogance and anger were gradually replaced by pangs of hunger, constant thirst, and intense fear. But still the dragons sat in silence, stubbornly refusing to make peace.

As time went on, the dragons' situation grew worse. Finally, an old and wise fire dragon broke the silence. "We have all behaved foolishly," he confessed. "We have wasted much time and energy for nothing. Who now is the greatest among us as we all sit here hungry and thirsty, shivering in the cold? King Benjamin often warned us of the dangers of living in a kingdom divided against itself—a kingdom where no one had respect for others. Now we are suffering because each of us chose not to listen to his warning. Our foolishness has cost us our beautiful land and has cost the king his magnificent palace. We must regain our honor. Enough of this foolishness, I tell you! Enough! If we are ever to overthrow King Jonus, the wicked ruler of Id, we must unite as one."

When the old dragon had finished speaking, he let out a tremendous roar and forced a huge ball of bright, orange fire from his mouth. Then in a show of unity, the entire colony of fire dragons joined in creating a roar so thunderous that it shook the very foundations of the cold, dark cave. Together, their fireballs were so enormous that they gave light to every inch of their mysterious and gloomy dwelling.

Then an amazing thing happened. Because the fire dragons had given light, the stone dragons were able to gather piles of stones just as they had done for the king. And because the fire dragons heated the stones, the hunters stopped shivering and were warm enough to hunt for food.

The hunter dragons began to explore the cave in search of food. As they searched, the hunters discovered that the mighty roar of the fire dragons had destroyed layers of the thick stone walls that led to a private storage chamber. In the chamber, to their surprise, they discovered a room stocked with plump animals dressed and ready for roasting. They had found King Jonus' private meat storage chamber! The hunters quickly gathered the fresh meat and returned to the others.

The hunter dragons shared the news of the secret chamber with the dragons who farmed the king's land. When the farmer dragons heard this news, they thought that if the king had meat stored in a secret place, he might also have food stored somewhere. They, too, then began to search the cave. Deeper and deeper they went. And finally, at the deepest part of the cave, they broke through a wall that unearthed a beautiful green garden nourished by the golden sun and a free-flowing stream.

The farmer dragons immediately gathered enough food for the entire colony. When they returned, they shared their news with the waterbearer dragons. They told them of the free-flowing stream they had found. Needing something to carry the water in, the waterbearers shared the news with the potter dragons and both groups went to the garden. When they reached the garden, they went right to the free-flowing stream. There they discovered enough thick red clay to make huge pots. So the potter dragons made the clay pots and the waterbearer dragons used them to gather water from the stream. Then they returned to the others.

When the potter and waterbearer dragons reached the others, they shared their news with the king's baker dragons. The bakers thought that if the hunters had found meat, the farmers had found food, the waterbearers had found water, and the potters had found clay to make pots, surely there must be something hidden for them to find. So the baker dragons began to search. Into the many tunnels of the cave they went until they, too, came across another chamber. This one was stocked with the finest ingredients available for baking bread. They quickly collected the ingredients, anticipating the sweet aroma and delicious taste of freshly baked bread. Then they returned to the others.

When the baker dragons reached the others, they shared the news of their discovery with the chariotmaker dragons. The chariotmaker dragons followed in the other dragons' footsteps and found yet another hidden chamber. This chamber was stocked with materials and tools used for building only the strongest and swiftest chariots. They quickly gathered the materials. Then they returned to the others and began their work of making chariots.

After eating, drinking, and finally making peace with each other, the Ogden dragons were no longer fearful. They felt strong and brave. The dragons were united. After the chariots were completed, the Ogden dragons created the perfect plan to reclaim their territory and free King Benjamin.

The dragons reasoned that if the roar of the fire dragons alone had dismantled several layers of the cave's stone walls, perhaps the roar of the entire colony would destroy the cave completely.

After finalizing their plans, the dragons arranged themselves in a circle against the thick stone walls of the cave. The wise old fire dragon gave the signal. At his command, the dragons looked toward the top of the cave and roared mightily while pushing on the cave's thick walls.

Slowly the walls of their once-cold and dark prison crumbled and crashed to the ground. The Ogden dragons were free! Boarding their swift newly-made chariots, they raced back to the Land of Ogden. Once there, they banded together and overthrew the wicked King Jonus. When they freed King Benjamin, the celebration began and they shared the story of their escape.

Kind and noble King, they began:

"The fire dragons gave us light that enabled the stone dragons to gather stones.

"The fire from the fire dragons warmed the stones gathered by the stone dragons.

"The warm stones helped the hunter dragons discover King Jonus' meat supply.

"The hunter dragons told the farmer dragons about their find, and the farmer dragons found the food supply.

"The farmer dragons told the waterbearer dragons and potter dragons about water near the food supply. The potter dragons found clay they could use to make pots for the waterbearer dragons to use to carry water.

"The potter dragons told the baker dragons, who found ingredients to make bread.

"The baker dragons told the chariotmaker dragons, who found materials to make swift chariots. And together, we escaped."

"Kind King Benjamin," they continued, "in the past, we chose not to listen to your warnings. But being captured by wicked King Jonus helped us learn many important lessons. Now we realize that though our jobs differ, each of us is equally important to the kingdom. And we have learned that it takes all of us to keep our kingdom strong and safe. Together, we regained our self-respect, and together, we learned to respect others. Together, we reclaimed our kingdom and freed you. We vow, King Benjamin, that there will be no more feuding in the Land of Ogden. We vow to live quietly and to roam freely in our land of peaceful streams and sun-kissed mountains."

"From this day forward," they proclaimed, "our kingdom will once again be known as Ogden, the land of beauty and peace."

 MAR*CO PRODUCTS, INC. © 2002 1-800-448-2197

DISCUSSION QUESTIONS

1. What did the Land of Ogden look like? *(There were peaceful streams, sun-kissed mountains, and thick forests.)*

2. Why did the dragons suddenly demand to live in separate colonies? *(Each group thought it was better than the others and did not want to associate with those who were not as good.)*

3. What kind of ruler was King Benjamin? *(He was kind.)*

4. How did he feel about the feuding? *(He disliked it and had trouble understanding why it was taking place.)* Did he warn against it? *(Yes.)*

5. What were some of the problems caused by the feuding? *(The dragons did not complete their chores and sometimes there was not enough food for them. Sometimes there was not enough food for King Benjamin.)*

6. What happened when King Jonus found out about the feuding? *(He conquered the country, imprisoned King Benjamin, and imprisoned the dragons.)*

7. How did the dragons learn their lesson? *(They were cold and hungry, and the wise old fire dragon told them that if they were to survive, they would have to help each other.)*

8. The dragons were very disrespectful of each other. Without using any names, can you tell about a time when you or someone you know was treated disrespectfully by others who felt they were the most important people? *(Accept any appropriate answers. Do not allow the students to mention any names.)*

9. How does being treated disrespectfully make someone feel? *(Accept any appropriate answers.)*

10. Does being different make a person unimportant? *(No.)*

SUPPLEMENTARY ACTIVITY

The Land Of Ogden: Distribute art paper and crayons to each student. Divide the students into three teams. Tell the first team to draw pictures of the Land of Ogden before the feuding, the second team to draw pictures of the Land of Ogden during the feuding, and the third team to draw pictures of the Land of Ogden after the feuding stopped. When the students have completed their drawings, assign one person from each team and form groups of three. Have the students share and explain their pictures. Begin with the student from the first team, follow with the second team, and conclude with the student from the third team. After each group has finished, ask the students to make a statement that will explain what they have learned from this lesson.

THE TRUTH IN THE BARN
GRADES 1-4

HONESTY

WRITTEN BY SHELLY ARNESON

Shelly Arneson is an elementary counselor in Florida.

THE TRUTH IN THE BARN

I knew there was something wrong when Rooster began howling in the middle of the day. Rooster is our collie, who wakes us every morning with a howl that sounds like a crow. That's why my sister, Kassie, named him Rooster. Kassie, who is seven years old, was in the kitchen. She was helping me make tuna fish sandwiches, when we heard Rooster.

I was trying to teach Kassie that the lump of tuna fish has to be spread on the bread. I would rather be outside doing work on the farm, but somebody has to take care of the meals and the rest of the housework. Mama used to do all that, but she got bone cancer five years ago and died just two years later.

I figure, at the age of 11, I've learned most of what it takes to run a house. I'm helping Kassie learn, too. Mama always used to say, "Joel, you'll make the world proud if you always do the right thing."

When Rooster let out a howl, Kassie looked at me with her wide brown eyes. "Joel," she said, "something's wrong with the puppies!"

We dropped the tuna and bread on the kitchen counter and ran outside. Rooster was jumping around. He ran toward the barn and then back to us, as if to say, "Hurry up! Henny's in trouble!" Henny is also our collie. She had just had a litter of five puppies.

I could see my dad coming from the field and running into the barn. Kassie and I raced toward the barn. My heart started beating faster than a hummingbird's.

Dad told us that when Henny had her puppies Kassie and I should leave them alone for a few days so Henny could take care of them. He told us that mother animals protect and feed their babies. But if they know humans have been around, they might desert their young. But yesterday, while Henny was out of the barn, I couldn't resist the urge to go in and take a look at her puppies. I knew I wasn't supposed to, but I just had to pick up one of the little pups. Besides, nobody saw me, not even Henny. So I supposed it must be all right.

When we stopped at the barn door, Dad was coming out. He had a look on his face that made my face feel like it was on fire. He looked at Kassie and me, and said, "Henny has pushed one of the pups out of the bed and won't feed her."

Kassie cried, "Oh, no! If Henny doesn't feed her, she'll die, won't she, Dad?"

Dad looked at me, adding heat to the fire already burning in my face. Then he turned to Kassie and said, "Yes, Baby, that's right. The puppies need their mama when they're first born. If Henny doesn't take care of her, she could die. Let's just hope Henny decides to pick up that puppy again and start feeding her. Now let's get back to work before it's time for lunch."

Dad headed back to the field. Kassie looked at me with trusting eyes, grabbed my hand, and said, "Come on, Joel. Let's go finish those sandwiches and hope Henny will take care of all her babies."

Just then, a huge lump formed in my throat. I had to tell the truth, if for no other reason than because Kassie trusted me. And Mama had trusted me to be a good and honest big brother to Kassie. I couldn't let them down.

"Dad!" I called out. Dad turned around. He had just reached the field, and I ran down to meet him.

I blurted out, "I have something to tell you. It's my fault Henny won't feed her baby. I went to see them yesterday and I picked one up. I thought as long as Henny didn't see me, it would be okay. Dad, is the puppy going to die because of me?" I asked, with tears streaming down my face.

Dad looked at me with love and concern in his eyes. He said, "No, son, I don't think Henny's going to let that one die. She is avoiding the pup right now because of the scent you left on her. If she doesn't start feeding it again, we'll get an eye dropper and you can feed the baby until it gets a little stronger."

"You've done the right thing by being honest," Dad continued. "I imagine you've learned a pretty powerful lesson, haven't you, Son?"

I thought about it for a moment and said, "I know now that I should always do the right thing, even when nobody's looking."

Dad looked down at me. I thought I saw tears in his eyes when he said, "Your mama would be so proud of you, Joel."

 MAR*CO PRODUCTS, INC. © 2002 1-800-448-2197

DISCUSSION QUESTIONS

1. What mistake did Joel make? *(He didn't listen to his father and picked up the newborn pup.)*

2. What was Joel's reason for needing to tell his dad the truth? *(He felt guilty for being dishonest, because his mother had always told him it was important to do the right thing.)*

3. How is this story similar to the one about George Washington and the cherry tree? *(Both boys did something they weren't supposed to do and both admitted their wrongdoing.)*

4. How does telling the truth help your relationship with your parents? With your teachers? With your friends? *(When you tell the truth, people know they can always count on you. Accept any other appropriate answers.)*

FOLLOW-UP ACTIVITIES

1. **Telephone:** Have five students line up and play the game of *Telephone*. The first person in line will whisper a statement (i. e., "We are going to eat pizza on Thursday if the sun is still shining.") to the next person in line. That person will then whisper the statement to the next person in line. This procedure will continue until the statement is whispered to the last person in line. The last person will then say the statement aloud. In most cases, the statement will not be the same as it was in the beginning. Discuss how this is like a lie—the more you pass it along, the more it will change. Discuss how a lie can harm a great many people.

   An alternate way to play the game would be to divide the class into five groups. Have one student from each group come to the front of the room. Then whisper the same statement to each student separately. When all of the students have heard the statement, they will return to their respective groups and follow the procedure above. It is interesting to see how many different endings can evolve from one statement.

2. **Consequences:** Select several magazine pictures. Think up a story about each picture. For example: Suppose you had a picture of a man talking on the telephone. You would show the picture to the students and say that the man is telling his boss that he can't come to work that day because he is sick. He is not really sick, but he wants to stay home. Have the students discuss what could happen as a result of his lie. Do this with each picture.

LUCIOUS LUDWIG LUDLOW, III
GRADES 1-3

HONESTY
FIBBING

WRITTEN BY WANDA S. COOK

Wanda Cook, a counselor in Texas, dedicates this story to the students at Thomas B. Francis Elementary School. She is also a contributor to the book *Special Situations,* published by Mar*co Products.

LUCIOUS LUDWIG LUDLOW, III

**There's a fellow that I know
Named Lucious Ludwig Ludlow, III
Who told the most ridiculous stories
That I have ever heard!**

To those in his presence,
Be they friend or foe or peer,
It seemed, without a doubt,
His fibs they would always hear.

As he began to speak,
Standing tall with a silly grin,
A twinkle in his eye
Signaled the lying would begin.

He seemed to have two favorite tales
It pleased him most to share.
Each was senseless and outrageous.
Take a listen, if you dare!

He claims the day he was born,
About a quarter past three,
He hopped from his crib
And slid down a tree.

Took the 4:10 bus,
Just as big as you please,
To a store by the shore
Owned by Mr. Ruiz.

By 5:15
He had made a gourmet meal
For his parents,
The nurses, and Doctor O'Neal.

When dinner was over and
He was cleaning up the dishes,
From a glass popped a genie
To grant him three wishes!

"My one and only wish," said he
Though three he'd gladly give,
"Was for the generous genie
To place me gently in my crib."

Then, he claims, at two years old,
He took a trip to the moon.
Departed in the morning,
And was back again by noon.

He says it took so much time
'Cause it's a mighty long flight
When your only transportation
Is a second-hand bike!

He tried to hitch a ride
On a south-bound comet.
But it zoomed by so close to him
He could only run from it.

The driver yelled with a sneer,
"All you Earthlings are alike!
And I don't give rides to a stranger
Who rides a second-hand bike!"

Lucious is now eight years-old
And things are not much better.
At least that's the message
His teacher sent his parents in a letter.

"TO THE PARENTS OF DEAR LUCIOUS:"
Is how the letter did start.
"To have to share this news with you
Really breaks my heart.

"Your son's constant fibbing
Has become a big distraction.
His sharing of silly tales
Makes *him* the center attraction.

"Today, during Language Arts,
His lies caused such a ruckus
I stopped teaching right away
And called Principal McStrukkus!"

Then finally Miss Nell wrote,
"We must devise a plan
To help dear Lucious learn
That if he tries, he can ...

"Learn the art of speaking truth.
And I hope you will agree
To sit with me and work this out
Tomorrow at half-past three."

Mom read the note to Lucious
And sternly to him said,
"Son, did this really happen?"
He said *yes* by nodding his head.

At school, I'm sometimes lonely.
It's friendship that I seek.
Then Mom bent down with teary eyes
And kissed his chubby cheek.

At the 3:30 meeting
Resolved Mom, Dad, and Miss Nell,
That when Lucious got the urge to lie
The Truth Squad he should tell.

Now this squad is a secret society
Of teachers and students who care,
Identified only by the letter "T"
And the bright smiles that they wear.

Mom explained the plan to Lucious
And he chose not a word to speak.
He simply rose when she was finished
And tenderly kissed her cheek.

Now Lucious was contented
And it pleased him so to know
That when he got the urge to fib,
To the Truth Squad he could go.

The first few weeks
Were hard, hard as they could be,
But when he wanted to tell a lie
He searched for a smile and a "T."

Soon, that twinkle left his eye
And he lost that silly grin.
You know, the one he would proudly sport
Before the fibbing would begin.

As time moved on, Lucious learned
This honored and valued lesson:
That old-fashioned honesty
Makes a wonderful impression.

It impressed Ingrid-Martha right away,
And dazzled Darci-Ruth.
"We like you so much better," said they,
"Since you've learned to tell the truth."

Their words echoed the thoughts
Of friends, and foes, and peers
Who liked to hear the truths he spoke
Instead of the lies they used to fear!

Now Lucious is helping others,
Like Little Molly Mae McClure.
She claims she created the common cold
And darn near has a cure.

So when you get the urge to lie,
Resist, and say what's true.
Seek out your very own Truth Squad
Just like Lucious chose to do.

DISCUSSION QUESTIONS

1. What type of problem did Lucious Have? *(He told fibs.)*

2. What is a fib? *(A fib is something that is not true, like a lie.)*

3. What two things did Lucious Ludwig Ludlow III lie about? *(He lied about the day he was born, and going to the moon when he was about two years old.)*

4. Did the students trust Lucious? *(No.)*

5. How did Lucious feel when fibbing to a big crowd? *(He felt happy, because he thought people were becoming his friends.)*

6. How did his parents and teacher feel about his constant fibbing? *(They were unhappy, disappointed, angry, etc.)*

7. Why did Lucious lie? *(He wanted to have friends.)*

8. What is the *Truth Squad,* and how did it help Lucious? *(In the story, it was a secret society that helped Lucious by encouraging him not to fib.)*

9. How did the children feel about Lucious after he stopped fibbing? *(They liked him better.)*

10. Who is Molly Mae McClure? *(She is a classmate Lucious is helping to stop fibbing.)*

FOLLOW-UP ACTIVITIES

1. **My Personal Truth Squad:** Reproduce *My Personal Truth Squad* (page 215) for any student who has difficulty with fibbing. Have each of these students complete the activity sheet during a personal conference, then form a Truth Squad using the people mentioned on the activity sheet.

2. **Lucious Ludwig Ludlow III Activity Puzzle:** Reproduce the *Lucious Ludwig Ludlow III Activity Puzzle* (page 216) for each student. Distribute a copy of the activity sheet and a pencil to each student. Have the students follow the directions and decode the secret message. The answer to the message is:

   The Truth Squad helped Lucious Ludwig Ludlow stop fibbing.

MY PERSONAL TRUTH SQUAD

Even though you know that fibbing is not good, (except when *not* fibbing might endanger your life or be harmful in any way) most of us fib at some time. Some of us fib too often. Look at the line below. Mark the place where you honestly think you fit.

NEVER FIB   **FIB SOMETIMES**   **FIB A LOT**

A Truth Squad is made up of people you trust. These are people you could go to whenever you feel the urge to tell a fib. They will listen to you and help you learn how not to fib. In the beginning, you may go to these people often. But as you get better and better at not fibbing, you will go to them less and less. In fact, you will eventually be able to close down your Truth Squad. And who knows? Maybe someday someone will want *you* as part of his or her Truth Squad!

MY TRUTH SQUAD

Person at home   _____

Adult at school   _____

Classmates   _____
(Pick 2 or 3)
_____

_____

LUCIOUS LUDWIG LUDLOW, III
ACTIVITY PUZZLE

Directions: Find the letter that matches the number and write the letter on the line above it. When you have finished, you will have decoded the secret message.

CODE:

A-1	B-2	C-3	D-4	E-5	F-6	G-7	H-8	I-9
J-10	K-11	L-12	M-13	N-14	O-15	P-16	Q-17	R-18
S-19	T-20	U-21	V-22	W-23	X-24	Y-25	Z-26	

___ ___ ___   ___ ___ ___ ___ ___
20 8   5   20 18 21 20 8

___ ___ ___ ___ ___   ___ ___ ___ ___ ___ ___
19 17 21 1   4   8   5   12 16 5   4

___ ___ ___ ___ ___ ___ ___
12 21 3   9   15 21 19

___ ___ ___ ___ ___ ___   ___ ___ ___ ___ ___ ___
12 21 4   23 9   7   12 21 4   12 15 23

___ ___ ___ ___   ___ ___ ___ ___ ___ ___ ___
19 20 15 16   6   9   2   2   9   14 7

CHARACTER-EDUCATION STORIES

CHARACTER-TRAIT STORIES
FOR
THE HOLIDAYS

TRAN OBEYS THE RULES
CITIZENSHIP DAY
(SEPTEMBER 17TH)

GRADES 3-5

CITIZENSHIP

WRITTEN BY ARDEN MARTENZ

Arden Martenz is a former teacher and elementary counselor from Pennsylvania.

 MAR*CO PRODUCTS, INC. © 2002 1-800-448-2197

TRAN OBEYS THE RULES

Kent and Tran were walking home from school when they saw a bottle along the side of the road. Tran picked it up and carried it to a trash can. Kent had seen Tran do this before. He wasn't sure why Tran went to so much trouble when people just kept throwing trash on the ground. But if he wanted to pick up after people, it was okay with Kent.

The boys had to cross a road. The signal was red, and Tran stopped on the curb. Kent looked both ways, saw that no cars were coming, and started across the street. "What are you doing?" yelled Tran. "Didn't you see the light?" "Sure," answered Kent, "but no cars are coming." "That doesn't make any difference! Get back on this curb!" Tran ordered. Kent really liked Tran, so he went back to the curb, even though he thought it made no sense at all to stand there while other people were crossing the street.

The next day, Mr. Boles gave a social studies assignment. He told the class they could do a report on anything about our country. Kent was excited, because *anything* meant he could write a report on the NFL football league. Football was Kent's favorite sport, and he wanted everyone to know about it. At lunch, Kent told Tran what he planned to write about and asked, "What are you doing your report on?" Tran matter-of-factly answered, "Immigration." Kent just looked at his friend. He didn't say anything, because he really wasn't sure what *immigration* was all about.

Two weeks went by. Tran kept picking up trash and stopping for red lights. Kent kept wondering if Tran was always going to act this way. Their reports were due the next day and, as the boys said good-bye in front of Tran's house, Kent asked, "Want to come over and shoot some hoops?" "Boy, I'd love to," answered Tran, "but I've got to go over my report for tomorrow. It's not quite finished, and I know Mr. Boles will call on me first." Kent thought to himself, "Well, that's Tran for you. He could have shot hoops and finished the report after dinner. But knowing him, I'm not surprised he wants to finish his schoolwork before he has any fun."

Tran was right. He was the first one called on to read his report. When Tran said, "My report is about immigration," you could see several classmates roll their eyes and settle down for a dull time. Kent felt bad for Tran because he knew when he got up and talked about the National Football League, everybody would sit up and be eager to listen. Then Tran began:

"Years ago, there was a war in Vietnam. I hadn't been born yet, but my father was a little boy. He lived in a village with my grandparents, aunts, and uncles. They didn't have a large house or much money. They were farmers, and they worked very hard to feed themselves. During the war, soldiers came through the villages. Sometimes, the soldiers took my family's food. There was a lot of shooting and bombing. Sometimes people in the village got killed, and sometimes the bombs destroyed houses and fields. When the fields were destroyed, there were no crops. Each day, my father woke up wondering if he would be alive or dead by nightfall.

"One day, the fighting came very close to the village. Bombs were falling and guns were shooting. My grandfather was afraid that everyone would be killed, so he told the family to run out of the house. They were afraid to leave. They were also afraid to stay. As the fighting came closer, they all fled. My father wasn't sure where he was going. He just ran along with his family and other people from their village. Some of the villagers dropped to the ground. They were wounded or dead. Then my father felt a sting. He stumbled and fell to the ground. His leg was bleeding. He had been shot. He tried to get up, but he couldn't. Just then, his father grabbed him and helped him run to safety in a ditch. When the fighting was over, my father and his father went back to their house. There was nothing left of it. In a little while, one of my aunts came back. They waited and waited, but my grandmother, my two uncles, and my other aunt never came back.

"My grandfather rebuilt the house and went back to work in the fields. The war was over, but the way of life was still hard. My father didn't want this kind of life forever, so he worked hard to come to America. When he was 25 years old, he married my mother. Then he had two people to bring to America. When they had enough money, they came over on a boat. My father went to school at night to learn English and washed dishes by day. My mother worked as a seamstress in a clothing factory. A year later, I was born. Now my father had to work even harder. He was not only washing dishes, but sweeping out buildings at night. He had to give up his classes in English, but he studied at night. I didn't know why he was reading so much until I heard my parents talking about him taking a test to become a *citizen*. I didn't know what that was. All I knew was that one day Mother cooked a great dinner because Dad was a United States Citizen.

"Being a citizen is a very important thing. When you are born in this country, you get for free what my father had to work years for. Sometimes people don't appreciate things that come too easily. I am a citizen because I was born here, but my father never lets me take my citizenship for granted. He has told me how important it is to obey all the laws and, when I get old enough, to vote. I know kids wonder why I pick up trash and why I won't cross the street if the light is red, but I do these things so I will be a good citizen. I don't want to forget how lucky I am to live in a country where I can go to school and not have to worry about bombs falling on my house.

"My father taught me to do what I can to make our country a better place. On September 17, we celebrate Citizenship Day. Our friends who have also become citizens get together for a big dinner and games. It's fun, but we all know the reason behind the celebration is the privilege of citizenship."

When Tran finished reading, the room was silent. Everyone had heard what he said, but no one could imagine the hardships his family had faced. Mr. Boles gave Tran a nod of approval and, as Tran started to his seat, the class broke into a round of applause. Kent gave his friend a high five as he walked by and whispered, "Bet I can pick up more trash than you on the way home from school!"

DISCUSSION QUESTIONS

1. Why did Kent think Tran was wasting his time picking up trash? *(Kent thought Tran was wasting his time because no matter how much trash Tran picked up, the area never stayed clean because people just continued to litter.)*

2. Where were Tran's parents born? *(They were born in Vietnam.)*

3. Who do you know who was born in another country? *(Accept any appropriate answers.)*

4. What holiday is this story about? *(This story about Citizenship Day, which is on September 17th.)*

5. Was it easy for Tran's father to become a citizen? *(No. He had to work hard to earn money to get to this country. And once he arrived here, he had to continue to work hard to earn money and study a lot to pass the citizenship examination.)*

6. Why was Tran a citizen? *(Tran was born in this country, which automatically made him a citizen.)*

7. What do you think the class learned from Tran's story? *(They learned about the importance of being able to be a citizen and reasons for following rules, such as waiting for the correct light before crossing a street. Accept any other appropriate answers.)*

8. What are some ways you can show good citizenship? *(Accept any appropriate answers.)*

SUPPLEMENTARY ACTIVITY

1. **How Rules Affect Other People:** Divide the students into groups. Give each group paper and a pencil. Tell each group to select a recorder to write down all of the group's ideas. Give each group one of the following titles: Rules Students Break At School, Rules Kids Break At Home, Rules People Break In The Community. When you have finished assigning the topics, tell the recorders to write down as many answers as the group can think of. When the groups have completed their lists, ask each group to read its answers. Record the answers on the chalkboard. Then discuss the consequences of breaking each of the rules and how doing so affects other people.

A NEW AND DIFFERENT WORLD
COLUMBUS DAY
(OCTOBER 12TH)

GRADES 3-5

TOLERANCE
FAIRNESS
JUSTICE

WRITTEN BY ARDEN MARTENZ

Arden Martenz is a former teacher and elementary counselor from Pennsylvania.

A NEW AND DIFFERENT WORLD

Cesar stood at the docks as he had done many times before. He loved his Spanish homeland, but there was something about a sailing ship that fascinated him beyond all else. He imagined what it would be like to be floating across the water, seeing new places, and meeting new people. He did not think that the seas might be rough or about any of the other dangers that went along with sailing. As an eight-year-old boy, he thought only of the adventure.

Thousands of miles away, another eight-year-old boy stood looking out to sea. Wakiza lived on an island. And although he went out into the water to help his father catch fish for food, he had often wondered what was beyond the barrier reef that his father was so careful not to venture past. He had never known anyone who had gone farther, and he had never seen any ships larger than his father's homemade canoe. Was there anything beyond the sea, or did it just go on forever? It was a question Wakiza never thought would be answered.

Cesar spent the next few years doing what he had always done. He helped his mother with chores, earned a small amount of money helping merchants, and watched the ships leave and return to the docks. His father was a baker, and his family was not wealthy. So school was not a part of Cesar's life. Going to school was a privilege reserved only for those whose families had money and influence. As he stood at the docks one day, he saw three ships: the Nina, Pinta, and Santa Maria. There had been talk around the docks for months that a sailor named Christopher Columbus had convinced the queen to finance a voyage to the Indies. Until now, ships sailing to the Indies always had made the long and treacherous voyage around Africa. Columbus was sure there was a shorter way. Others weren't as sure, but Queen Isabella had faith in him and granted him three ships and 88 men. It was these men Cesar saw standing in line to sign on for the voyage.

Cesar saw something else that day. He saw a boy about his age standing on the deck of one of the ships. Cesar watched the boy for a long time. When the boy finally came onto the dock, Cesar asked him his name and what he was doing. The boy told Cesar he was a cabin boy. He explained that someday he wanted to be a captain of a ship, just like Columbus. Until he was old enough to be a sailor, he worked as a cabin boy, doing errands and simple jobs.

"I could do that," thought Cesar. "I could do that, and then I could go to sea." But then he thought about his parents and what they would say if he went off to a place no one knew. That night was a long night at Cesar's house, as he tried desperately to convince his parents to let him become a cabin boy. He used every argument he could think of, and still his parents would not agree. The next morning, Cesar's father saw him sitting outside looking toward the docks. His father sat down beside him and told Cesar he had thought about it all night long. He was frightened for Cesar. But he also knew that when he was a boy, he had dreams, too. But his dreams were never fulfilled. Cesar looked at his father. His father just nodded and pointed toward the docks. It was a dream come true! Cesar jumped up and ran as fast as he could, not speaking to anyone. He was on his way to the docks. When he arrived, there was no line. The ships were standing still. Cesar was about to give up hope when he saw a tall man standing on deck. He waved and yelled until the man saw him and, after boarding the ship, and talking for what seemed like hours, Cesar became a cabin boy.

The voyage was not everything Cesar had expected. There were rough seas, which made him sick to his stomach. The food was not as good as his mother's and, as time went on, both food and water became scarce and had to be rationed. Columbus was sure of his course, but his sailors were not. They began to become frightened and demanded to go back to Spain. Cesar watched Columbus. He believed Columbus was a fair and just man, because he bargained with his crew to sail for two more days. If nothing was sighted by then, Columbus agreed to turn back to Spain. But they did not turn back, because two days later, the crew spotted birds. Knowing birds had to be near land, they followed them and sighted what Columbus believed to be the Indies. Of course, nothing could have been further from the truth. Columbus had reached a new world!

From that day forward, both Cesar and Wakiza's lives changed. An excited Columbus dressed in his finest clothes, went ashore, kissed the ground, and claimed the land for Spain. Cesar could not believe what he was seeing. Neither could Wakiza. He was hiding in the bushes with his fellow tribespeople and looking at a ship larger than any he had ever seen and at a man, dressed in strange clothes, kissing the ground. He and his fellow tribespeople decided that Columbus and his men must be gods. Believing this, they came out to meet Columbus and his men. They welcomed the strangers into their homes and treated them royally.

Cesar and Wakiza became friends. Wakiza taught Cesar to hunt for snakes, turtles, and iguanas. Cesar wished he could teach Wakiza something, but the land was strange and he could not think of anything he knew that Wakiza would want to learn. When the boys met, they would try to talk to each other, but neither of them understood the other. They would point and make funny movements with their bodies, trying to tell each other what they meant. Each time they did this, they said words. Soon each of them was learning the other's language. To the boys, this was great. Now not only could they be with each other, but each of them could understand what the other was trying to say.

Columbus believed there was gold to be found in this new land, and he wanted to take it back to the queen. He also wanted to convert the Indians, a name he gave the people because he believed he had reached the Indies, to Christianity. To find the gold, he needed to explore nearby islands. To do this, he needed guides. Columbus was aware of the friendship between Cesar and Wakiza and when he selected guides, he forced Wakiza to become one of them. Wakiza didn't want to go. He didn't want to leave his island. Cesar did not know what to do. He couldn't defy Columbus. He wanted to tell him that Wakiza wanted to stay with his people. But in his heart, Cesar believed that Columbus already knew that. Columbus knew that none of the six guides he had selected wanted to be with him. To Cesar, this did not make sense. Where was the fairness that Cesar had seen Columbus display to his men when they wanted to return to Spain? Why wasn't he being fair to Wakiza and his fellow tribesmen?

During Columbus' search for gold, the Santa Maria ran aground on a reef and had to be abandoned. Columbus decided it was time to return to Spain. Wakiza was happy, because now he could return to his island. But his happiness was short-lived. Columbus decided to take the six guides back to Spain. Cesar didn't know why Columbus felt this was a good idea, but as usual, he was afraid to question Columbus.

Cesar did not see Wakiza after he returned to Spain. He returned to his parents' home and told them of his voyage and of his confusion about why some people were treated differently than others. Cesar's parents listened to his stories, but they had no answer for him. All they could say was, "That's just the way it is." Cesar began to think there was no answer to his question, but he could not help thinking about it.

Cesar was walking around the docks one day when he heard two sailors say that Columbus was going back to sea. He wanted to return to the islands he had found earlier. Cesar, although upset over the way the Indians had been treated, still loved the sea and really was not trained to earn a living in any other way. It didn't take much questioning to find out where and when Columbus was sailing, and Cesar went to the docks to see if there was a place for him. "You're too old to be a cabin boy, Cesar," his sailor friend told him. "But you've been to sea and Columbus knows you. Why don't you see about signing on as one of the crew?" Cesar had not thought of being one of the crew. But he knew, if he wanted to be a sea captain some day, this was the place to start. So Cesar went back to sea with Columbus, to the island they had left behind.

Wakiza was on board the ship. His knowledge of both languages made him a valuable addition to the voyage. But it did not make him equal. Cesar hardly saw Wakiza. And when he did see him, Cesar wasn't usually able to speak with him. His friend had changed. Wakiza wasn't the happy person that Cesar had known on the island. He was quiet, and he had become frail and sickly. Cesar wondered what had happened to Wakiza.

What had happened was disease. Wakiza wasn't immune to the diseases of Spain, and he was very ill. His spirit was broken. By the time the ships landed in the Indies, Wakiza was so ill that Columbus had him taken to his village. This probably seemed like a good idea. But just as Wakiza was not immune to the diseases of Spain, neither were the other Indians. Many became sick and died.

One day, Cesar was able to leave the ship and visit Wakiza. The two were finally alone and were able to talk freely. Wakiza told Cesar of the treatment he received in Spain, and Cesar kept telling him that it wasn't fair. Cesar told his friend that he wished there were something he could do to help. Wakiza told Cesar there was nothing he could do and that he should not feel guilty. Wakiza also said that he knew Cesar was a good person who would not treat others in the way that his tribe was being treated. When Cesar left Wakiza, he felt better because they had had a chance to talk and because Wakiza knew that he wasn't like the others. But he felt worse because he knew that there was nothing he could do to change the situation. He had no power. And in those days, if you didn't have power, your voice would not be heard.

Cesar returned to the ship. Before it left for Spain, he learned that Wakiza had died. When he heard this he felt a part of him had died, too. As he looked over the ship's railing at the land, the island did not have the same meaning for him as it had once had. He knew then what his decision would be.

The ship returned to Spain and Cesar returned to his family. He never went to sea again. Instead, he joined his father in the bakery and made bread for a living. At times, he would return to the docks and listen to the sailors' stories. He learned that Columbus had sailed twice more after Cesar left the ship. He heard tales of beatings and murders, ransacking villages, starvation, and slavery. Each story made Cesar remember what a friendly and happy people the Indians had been before he and Columbus entered their land.

The voyages to the Indies haunted Cesar throughout his life. He knew that Columbus and his determination resulted in a new world being encountered. And this was a good thing. For today, this new world houses many people who enjoy many freedoms. He also knew that he could not change the way the world was in 1492, but he could change the way he acted and believed. Cesar vowed always to be fair to everyone of every age, sex, race, or religion. He also vowed to be tolerant of the beliefs of others and to make just decisions. These were vows he lived by and never broke throughout his lifetime.

DISCUSSION QUESTIONS

1. Why did Cesar believe Columbus to be a fair and just man? *(He believed Columbus was fair and just because he listened to his crew and compromised with them.)*

2. What did Wakiza and Cesar do for each other? *(They taught each other their languages.)*

3. What caused Cesar to question Columbus' fairness? *(He saw that Columbus tried to treat his crew fairly, but did not treat the Indians in the same manner.)*

4. Why didn't Cesar question Columbus' treatment of the Indians? *(In those days, freedom of speech was not what it is today. If you were a person of power, people listened to you. But Cesar was not a person of power. Besides, he believed Columbus already knew that Wakiza and the others did not want to go with him.)*

5. How do you think Wakiza felt when he had to go with Columbus? *(Accept any appropriate answers.)*

6. Why did Cesar change his mind about going to sea again? *(He did not want to be a part of the way the Indians were being treated.)*

7. How did going to sea change Cesar's life? *(He vowed to always be fair, tolerant, and just to everyone regardless of their race, religion, creed, or sex. He kept this vow throughout his life.)*

SUPPLEMENTARY ACTIVITY

1. **Cooperative Learning Activity:** Divide the students into five groups and give each group paper and a pencil. Assign each group one of the following questions:

    *   Why was Columbus' voyage a good thing?

    *   Why wasn't Columbus tolerant of the Indians and their beliefs?

    *   What do you think the Indian guides thought and felt when they reached Spain?

    *   What do you think would have happened to Cesar if he had expressed his opinions to Columbus?

    *   How do you think Cesar kept his vows as a baker?

Tell the groups to elect a secretary to write down their ideas, a leader to keep the group on task, and a spokesperson to relate their ideas to the rest of the class. Tell the students how much time the groups will have to formulate their ideas. When the allotted time has elapsed, tell the groups they must work together and select five ideas to present to the class. No group may present more than five ideas. After all the presentations have been made, if time allows, have those students who wish to do so contribute additional comments.

POLITICS! ELECTIONS! VOTING!
ELECTION DAY
(SECOND TUESDAY IN NOVEMBER)
PRIMARY ELECTIONS

GRADES 2-5

CITIZENSHIP
PATRIOTISM

WRITTEN BY ARDEN MARTENZ

Arden Martenz is a former teacher and elementary counselor from Pennsylvania.

 MAR*CO PRODUCTS, INC. © 2002 1-800-448-2197

POLITICS! ELECTIONS! VOTING!

"I've had it," Mindy yelled as she stomped into the kitchen. "I wait all week to see my TV show, and then some person running for governor comes on to give a speech and my program is gone. It's not fair."

"Want to bake some cookies?" her mother asked.

"No, I don't want to do anything. I hate those politicians," Mindy answered as she stormed off to her room.

A few hours later, Mother called Mindy for dinner. As everyone sat around the table, Dad mentioned that the President had made a statement about maybe having to send troops to a foreign country Mindy had never heard of. Jill, Mindy's older sister, immediately joined in the conversation. Jill said that there had been a big discussion about this topic in her social studies class that day. Then, of course, Mom also had to say what *she* thought.

"How boring," Mindy thought as she kept on eating. Mom had made mashed potatoes, and they were Mindy's favorite. All this talk about politics just made her remember she hadn't seen her favorite TV show. But no matter. She could forget about anything as long as there were mashed potatoes. In fact, another helping would be in order right now. But as luck would have it, just as Mindy went to reach for the bowl, her brother, Ron, picked it up and scraped it clean.

"That does it!" cried Mindy. "All this family talks or cares about is politics. We can't even eat dinner without you talking about it. And Mom, you can't even make enough for us to eat."

"That's enough, Mindy," her father interrupted. "If you don't know how to act at the dinner table, you can go to your room."

"But ..." Mindy started to protest.

"Now, Mindy, now! Go to your room," her father said in a voice that told Mindy that arguing wasn't a choice. Her room was where she had to go.

The next day, Jill was sitting out by the family pool. Mindy came out and started to go into the water. The day was hot and humid, and cooling off was the only thing on Mindy's mind.

"If anyone needs to cool off, it's you," said Jill.

"Why do you say that?" asked Mindy.

"After that scene you made at dinner," replied Jill.

"Well, I'm sick of all this political stuff. It's taking my shows off TV, everyone talks about it at dinner, and Ron ate all the mashed potatoes," whined Mindy.

"Ron ate all the mashed potatoes? What that has to do with anything, I don't know. But I do know you should have been born 200 years ago. Then you wouldn't have had to worry about politics," said Jill.

"What in the world are you talking about?" asked Mindy.

"Well, 200 years ago, women couldn't vote. So politics meant nothing to them. Not many women were able to get an education, and those who worked had few career choices and were paid less money than men who did the same job. There weren't many women brave enough to speak up for women, and those who did were laughed at. One of those women was Susan B. Anthony. She believed women should have the right to vote, just like men. She went throughout the country giving speeches. She believed so much that women should have the right to vote that she spent 60 of her 86 years working to gain that right for them."

"I'll bet she was really happy when she voted," said Mindy.

"Wrong," replied Jill. "She never did vote. She died before they passed the amendment allowing women to vote."

"What a gyp that was," Mindy answered.

"I guess you could say that," Jill continued. "But without her efforts, who knows how long it would have been before women had the same rights as men or even whether we'd have them today. Other women kept her fight for equal rights going and are still doing so today. So you see, when you complain about politics, you really are complaining about something we worked very hard to achieve—the right to have a say in politics—the right to vote."

"It all has to do with being a good citizen and being patriotic," Jill went on. "For example, would you take our garbage and throw it on Mr. and Mrs. Lyons' lawn?"

"Don't be ridiculous," Mindy said in a huff. "Of course not. I know better than to litter."

"Okay," Jill said. "Then would you tell people you live in a rotten country?"

Now Mindy was getting angry. "Jill, what's wrong with you? I know about being a good citizen, and I know about being patriotic. I'm not stupid, you know."

"Of course you're not," agreed Jill. "And that's why you can easily figure out that being interested in political issues makes Mom and Dad better-informed citizens and voters. It shows they don't take for granted the privileges a lot of people worked hard to gain."

Mindy settled down and asked, "Do you think most girls think about the things you're telling me?"

"I really don't know," answered Jill. "But so you will remember to think about them, I have a present for you."

"Really?" asked Mindy excitedly.

Then Jill handed Mindy a coin. On it was the picture of a woman.

"What's this?" asked Mindy.

"It's a Susan B. Anthony dollar," replied Jill. "As of now, she is the only woman to be on a United States coin. And next February, when you get excited about Valentine's Day, remember that the next day, February 15th, is Susan B. Anthony Day."

"I'm never going to spend this dollar. And next time I see a woman who is trying to win an election or a woman who is already a congresswoman, senator, governor, or in any other office, I'll remember Susan B. Anthony," Mindy announced as she put her dollar in her purse.

"Are you going to remember anything else?" asked Jill.

"Yes," answered Mindy. "Even though I may not understand all of the political things Mom and Dad get so excited about, I will remember that without Susan B. Anthony and others like her, women would not have the rights of citizenship that they have today."

DISCUSSION QUESTIONS

1. Do you think most kids your age think politics are boring? Why or why not? *(Accept any appropriate answers. Expand on those answers that would make the reasons clearer.)*

2. Would Mindy have been as upset about the dinner-table conversation if she had been able to get more mashed potatoes? *(Accept any appropriate answers. Have the students explain the reasons for their beliefs.)*

3. How was Susan B. Anthony honored by our country? *(Her image is on a coin and February 15th is recognized as Susan B. Anthony Day.)*

4. Do you think many people know about this holiday? Why or why not? *(Accept any appropriate answers.)*

5. Was it easy for Susan B. Anthony to enlist support for her cause? *(No. She was laughed at and people did not take her seriously.)*

6. How did Susan B. Anthony feel when she was able to vote? *(She never did vote. She died 14 years before the Nineteenth Amendment was passed.)*

7. Why is voting an example both of patriotism and citizenship? *(Voting demonstrates that you want a voice in how our country is run and take seriously your opportunity to elect the officials who run our country. Voting also demonstrates that you think enough of your country to participate in an event that will affect you and every other person living in our country.)*

8. You are not old enough to vote. What are some things you do to demonstrate good citizenship? *(Accept any appropriate answers.)*

SUPPLEMENTARY ACTIVITY

1. **Segregation:** Tell the students that instead of having classroom jobs assigned to them, they will have the opportunity to vote for the jobs they want to do. If necessary, have the class brainstorm about the jobs to be voted for and write their suggestions on the chalkboard. If it is not necessary to brainstorm about the jobs, write the usual classroom jobs on the chalkboard. Give each student paper and a pencil. Tell each of the students to select one or two jobs he/she would like to do for the next two weeks. Collect the papers. Then look at the papers and write one or two boys' names after each job listed on the chalkboard. If no boy has signed up for a job, ask for volunteers to fill the position. Explain to the class that even though the girls would like to have jobs and would probably do them well, it's only permissible for boys to hold classroom jobs. Then distribute paper to the boys in the classroom. Tell the boys to vote for their choices, explaining again that it's only permissible for boys to vote. When the boys have finished voting, ask the students to explain how they feel about what has just happened.

   This activity can be extended by having the boys do the jobs for two weeks and then discussing how both the boys and the girls feel about the situation.

A COMMON BOND
THANKSGIVING DAY
(FOURTH THURSDAY IN NOVEMBER)

GRADES 2-5

TOLERANCE
PREJUDICE REDUCTION

WRITTEN BY ARDEN MARTENZ

Arden Martenz is a former teacher and elementary counselor from Pennsylvania.

A COMMON BOND

The first winter had been hard for the Colony in Massachusetts. Over one-half of the settlers who had come to the New World had died during the coldest months. When Spring came and it was time for planting, the Colonists' seed came from a new source: the Native American Wampanoag Tribe that resided nearby. These peoples, mistakenly called *Indians* by Columbus (who thought he had landed in India when he really had landed in the islands off North America), had come to the aid of the Colony and given them seed to plant. Spring and Summer were kind to the crops, and there was a good harvest. Thankful for this good harvest, the Colonists planned a celebration. Because they were grateful for the help given by their Wampanoag neighbors, the Colonists invited the Wampanoag to attend the celebration.

Sarah was a young girl who lived in the Massachusetts Colony. Her father was a *cooper*. That meant he made barrels. Her father's job was important, because barrels were what the Colonists used to store grains and other essential items.

The Thanksgiving feast was exciting for Sarah. Her mother was busy helping prepare food, like all of the women in the Colony. Some of the men fished for cod and bass and others hunted for wildfowl. It was to be a really great day. There was only one thing that Sarah wasn't sure about: The Wampanoag!

The day before the feast, Sarah was helping her mother. They talked as they worked, and Sarah's mother could tell that something was bothering her daughter.

"Sarah, are you all right?" asked her mother.

"Yes, Mother, I'm all right," Sarah replied.

"Then why are you putting the food back into the barrel instead of onto the plates? It seems as if your mind is somewhere other than here," Mother noted.

"I'm sorry. I guess I was thinking about something else," Sarah said apologetically. "I'm excited about tomorrow, but I really don't like the idea that the Wampanoag are coming."

"But, Sarah, this isn't like you. You know how much they helped us," Mother replied.

"I know. But they dress funny, I don't understand what they're saying most of the time, and they have that reddish-brown skin. They're so different. I like people who are like us."

Milala was a young girl who was a member of the Wampanoag Tribe. Her father was a hunter. He spent a lot of time searching the woods for game for his family and for other members of the tribe. He also made canoes from birch bark.

The upcoming feast was confusing for Milala. She was used to her tribe's celebrations, and she always looked forward to them. But this was different. They were going somewhere else. That was all right, but there was one thing that she wasn't sure about: The white people!

The day before the feast, Milala was helping her mother. They talked as they worked, and Milala's mother could tell that something was bothering her daughter.

"Milala, are you all right?" asked her mother.

"Yes, Mother, I'm all right," Milala replied.

"Then why are you putting the baskets of food in a place where the animals can get at them? It seems as if your mind is somewhere other than here," Mother noted.

"I'm sorry. I guess I was thinking about something else," Milala said apologetically. "I'm excited about tomorrow, but I really don't like the idea that we're going over to be with the white people."

"But, Milala, this isn't like you. You know how grateful they are for the seed we gave them," Mother replied.

"I know. But they dress funny, I don't understand what they're saying most of the time, and they have that white skin. They're so different. I like people who are like us."

The day of the feast arrived. The Colonists had bowls of vegetables, wildfowl, and fish. The Wampanoag brought venison. It was a wonderful day for feasting and games.

Sarah watched as the Wampanoag came into the clearing. They looked friendly enough, but Sarah wasn't about to be taken in by their friendly looks. After all, everybody knew that they didn't know enough to build decent homes or wear decent clothes.

Milala walked into the clearing with her family. She stayed close to her mother as she looked around at the waiting white people. They looked friendly enough, but Milala wasn't about to be taken in by their friendly looks. After all, everybody knew that they didn't know how to hunt in the forest, and who knew if they could even dance and sing like the Wampanoag could?

One day went by, and the next, and it was the third day of the feast. Most of the children were playing games, but not Sarah and Milala. Each had her own doll and sat away from the others, playing alone. The boys were playing ball nearby. Then it happened! The ball the boys were playing with rolled over in front of Sarah. Milala's brother yelled, "Milala, get the ball and throw it back."

Milala didn't move. "Milala," yelled her brother. "Hurry up! Get the ball and throw it back." Milala looked at her brother. Then she looked at the white girl. She was sitting there, holding her doll, and looking at Milala, then looking at the ball.

Milala got up slowly. She looked at the ground. She didn't want to look at the white girl. If she ran fast and threw the ball, she could get it over quickly and get away from the white girl. Milala started to run. She ran to the ball. But when she bent over to pick it up, she dropped her doll. It fell right in front of the white girl. Milala threw the ball, then looked for her doll.

Milala's doll wasn't on the ground. The white girl had picked it up. Now Milala would probably have to fight the white girl to get it back. Then her parents and even the chiefs of the tribe would be angry. She didn't know what to do, but she *did* know that she wanted her doll back.

Sarah looked at the Wampanoag girl's doll. It was different from hers. It was made from tree bark. Sarah had never seen a doll like this. It didn't have a dress, and the face was painted on. Sarah laid her doll down while she examined Milala's doll more closely. Then she noticed two moccasin-clad feet in front of her. When Sarah looked up, she saw Milala, looking down at her. The girls looked at each other. Each had the same thoughts: She looks friendly. She's about the same size as I am. We both play with dolls.

Sarah started to hand Milala's doll back to her when she noticed Milala looking at her doll. Sarah, for a reason she couldn't explain, handed her own doll to Milala. Milala looked at it and sat down by Sarah. Soon the two girls began showing each other different things. Milala showed Sarah a beaded bracelet, and Sarah showed Milala a necklace with a gold locket. This continued until the girls were called to eat. They walked toward the tables laden with food. When the girls reached the table, Sarah sat down on a bench. Milala had never sat on a bench. She always sat on the ground. She looked at Sarah, who pointed to the space next to her and motioned for Milala to sit down. Milala wasn't sure what to do. She looked over and saw her mother nod approval. And so Milala sat down and ate her first meal from a table. She thought to herself, "Next time, Sarah should eat sitting on the ground with me."

At the end of the third day, when they had all finished eating, the Wampanoag got ready to return to their camp. Milala joined her family and started to walk toward the forest. She turned back and saw Sarah standing at the edge of the clearing and waving to her. "I guess that means *good-bye*," thought Milala, and so she waved back.

DISCUSSION QUESTIONS

1. How were the girls feeling at the beginning of the story? *(They were not happy about being around people who were different from them.)*

2. Why were they so worried about being with persons of a different culture? *(They had never had contact with people who dressed differently from them or who spoke another language.)*

3. What happened to bring Sarah and Milala together? *(Milala dropped her doll in front of Sarah.)*

4. How were the girls feeling at the end of the story? *(They were friendly toward each other.)*

5. Do you think the girls will now feel differently about people of different cultures? Why? *(Yes. Accept any appropriate answers.)*

FOLLOW-UP ACTIVITIES

1. **What If?:** Make up *What If ...* statements:

   What if ...
   everyone treated everyone else equally?
   no one ever called another person a name?
   fighting was not a part of our culture?
   weapons had never been invented?
   everyone in the world spoke a different language?
   no one was ever excluded from a game because they do not play well?

   Divide the students into groups. Give each group a slip of paper with a *What If ...* statement written on it, a piece of chart paper, and pencils. Tell the students to write all of the answers they can think of to their statement on the chart paper. Tell the students how much time they have to complete the activity. When the allotted time has elapsed, have each group share its conclusions.

2. **Sentence Completion:** Ask each student to complete the following sentence stem aloud:

   "One way I can show more tolerance is to _____."

ABRAHAM
PRESIDENTS' DAY
(THIRD MONDAY IN FEBRUARY)

GRADES 1-5

PATIENCE
PERSEVERANCE

WRITTEN BY ARDEN MARTENZ

Arden Martenz is a former teacher and elementary counselor from Pennsylvania.

ABRAHAM

Abraham **was just a little boy.** He wasn't even old enough to go to school, but he had to help around the farm. No one on a farm sat around and watched other people work. Everyone had to do chores. During planting season, Abraham had to help plant seeds. During harvest season, he had to help pick the fruits and vegetables. All year long, he chopped wood, carried water, and built fires in the hearth. It was not an easy life, but little Abraham knew what was expected of him. He learned to be a hard worker.

When Abraham was six years old, an exciting thing happened. He was allowed to go to school! You see, in those days not everyone went to school. Nobody told children they had to learn to read and write and not everyone learned to do those things. Many people spent their entire lives never being able to read anything or write anything down. So when Abraham was allowed to go to school, he was excited. He didn't know what to expect the first day when he and his older sister, Sarah, trudged two miles down the road to reach the little schoolhouse. Every day after that became a new and exciting adventure. Abraham was learning to read! He was learning to write! He was learning to do math!

Homework was never a problem for Abraham. He was so eager to learn that no one ever had to remind him to practice his subjects. But Abraham's family was very poor and could not afford to buy slates or paper for his schoolwork. Without supplies to practice his handwriting, Abraham could have given up and said there was no way he could ever learn. But he didn't. There was no way he was going to give up something he wanted so much. He took charcoal from the hearth and practiced his writing on the back of a shovel. He even practiced by writing in the dust and snow. Nothing would stop him from reaching his goals. He was a very determined six-year-old boy.

Although Abraham's chores and schooling kept him busy most of the time, whenever he could he would leave the farm and roam through the nearby forest, wade in a creek, and climb the cliffs. He would often stand on the top of the cliffs and watch the wagons roll westward.

Abraham's schooling did not last very long. When he was seven years old, his family left Kentucky and moved to Indiana. Now, Abraham had to help his father cut a trail through the wilderness so they could get to the place where they would build their home. The winter was very cold, and all they had time to build was a shed with one side open. To keep warm, they had to burn a fire night and day. In the spring, Abraham helped his father build a log cabin. One of his other chores was to go with his sister to pick wild berries, nuts, and fruit. He had to walk a mile to fetch water and carry it back to the house. Life was not much fun for Abraham, but he knew that he had responsibilities. He did what was expected of him.

Shortly after the family moved to Indiana, Abraham's mother died. Sarah took over all the household chores. Before long, his father remarried. Abraham's stepmother was a kind woman who moved into the little house with her own three children and made it into a home. She encouraged Abraham to study.

When Abraham was eleven years old, he went back to school. He had been reading as much as he could since leaving Kentucky, but now he would actually have someone to teach him. In those days, teachers did not stay very long in one place. They would come to an area, stay for a couple of weeks, and then move on. This meant that Abraham did not really go to school for very long, because when one teacher left, he would have to wait for another one to come by. But Abraham was not discouraged. He walked the four miles to and from school when the teacher was there and studied on his own when there was no teacher at the school.

In his whole life, Abraham's total schooling added up to about one year. Yet he never gave up. He always worked hard. By the time he was fifteen years old, he was working as a hired hand on a farm. He kept a book tucked inside his shirt so he could read whenever he had a few free minutes. When he was eighteen years old, he built a scow and earned money by rowing passengers across the Ohio River. He was also a postmaster and worked as a surveyor and as a storekeeper while studying to be a lawyer. Then he went into politics. He became a congressman and, eventually, the sixteenth president of the United States.

Abraham Lincoln is best known for abolishing slavery in the United States. He was a man who, as a young boy, learned that if he wanted something enough, he had to be patient and never allow himself to be swayed from his course of action.

DISCUSSION QUESTIONS

1. What did Abraham want most of all? *(He wanted to learn.)*

2. How do you know that Abraham was patient? *(He did not become discouraged when a teacher left his school and he had to wait for another to arrive.)*

3. How do you know that Abraham persevered? *(Even when he wasn't in school, he would have a book tucked in his shirt and read whenever he had free time.)*

4. How do you think Abraham felt when he had to work so hard? *(Accept any appropriate answers.)*

5. If you were not allowed to come to school, how do you think you would learn? *(Accept any appropriate answers.)*

SUPPLEMENTARY ACTIVITY

1. **Achieving A Goal:** Ask the students to name the different things they do during the day. Write their answers on the chalkboard. Then review the list and cross out all of the things the students do but that Abraham would not have been able to do. Then have the students complete the following sentence stem:

    "One thing I want as badly as Abraham wanted an education is _____."

    Distribute paper and a pencil to each student. Ask the students to write a story about how they can get the one thing they want as badly as Abraham wanted an education. In their story, they may use only the things that remain on the chalkboard as ways of achieving their goals.

THE THEYS
EARTH DAY
(CLOSE TO OR ON APRIL 22ND)

GRADES 3-5

RESPECT FOR THE ENVIRONMENT

WRITTEN BY ARDEN MARTENZ

Arden Martenz is a former teacher and elementary counselor from Pennsylvania.

THE THEYS

It was only a small piece of land—not a forest—but it had several trees and a small stream. You could call it a *glen*. Because it was small, all of the trees, the flowers, and the stream knew each other well. They had been neighbors for many years and each cared a great deal for the others. Together, they had survived hot and dry summers, cold and icy winters, thunderstorms, and heavy winds.

"Here *They* come again," cried Weeping Willow. "Oh, my, I hope they pass me by. I don't want any more of my branches broken off. It hurts too much."

"I really wouldn't mind if *They* climbed on me," said Apple Tree, "but *They* break off my little branches and use them for sticks. It's too much to bear."

"What is wrong with you?" asked Big Oak. "You guys just get too attached to your branches. Then when something happens to them, you get upset. Now in my case, I really have a problem. I need my acorns so other oak trees can grow. I don't mind losing some of them for decorations, but when *They* throw them at each other and smash them, I just wish I could ... I wish I could ... I wish I could do something, but I don't know what."

"Right," said Running Stream. "*They* always go away, but not before they throw trash into me. I work so hard to have clean, clear water. Then all my work goes down the drain, so to speak, when *They* come."

"Sure, you have problems, but what about us?" questioned the Wildflowers. "*They* pick us and throw us away and when *They* run, *They* trample us down so badly that we can never stand up straight again."

Just then, Spring Breeze blew into the little glen. Listening to the problems, she added, "You don't know how good you have it. I've just come from blowing around a group of smoking *Theys*. When I started to come near them, my air was fresh and full of good oxygen. Then when it got around them, it was all over. My air smelled bad. It wasn't the good clean air I had when I started my day. You don't know how good you have it to be able to live here and only get bothered by the *Theys* once in a while. I'm moving constantly, and I have problems with the *Theys* almost every day of my life."

The trees, the water, the flowers, and the air understood each other's problems, even though it sounded like they only cared about what happened to themselves. They really cared about each other, and they knew they were helpless to do anything about the *Theys*.

The noise grew louder. *They* were getting closer. The trees, water, flowers, and air could hear the sounds of their laughter and the noises *They* made with their voices. The noises were strange, but *They* seemed to understand each other. Soon the *Theys* came into view. Only this time, it wasn't the usual group. This time, *They* were big and little, six in all. *They* were carrying a basket and it looked like they were carrying lots of other things, too.

When *They* reached the glen, the trees, water, flowers, and air didn't understand what was happening. What was this strange mixture? *They* were always the same size and *They* just ran around and jumped and climbed on everything. It was hard to believe that *They* came in different sizes. So the trees, water, flowers, and air watched very carefully.

One of the big *Theys* laid something down on the grass and the little ones began sitting on it. Another of the big *Theys* set the basket down and started taking things out of it. This was all very strange. And soon it became even more strange.

Running Stream saw the little *Theys* coming toward her. "See? I told you so! Here comes the trash. I wonder what *They* will throw in me this time?" Running Stream said to the trees and flowers. But the little *Theys* only splashed and played in the water. *They* didn't throw any trash. *They* just had fun. Running Stream laughed when she saw how the little *Theys* were having fun and not ruining her water.

The trees, air, and flowers watched as Running Stream laughed. They couldn't believe what they saw. Just then, one little *They* came toward the flowers. "Oh, no," said Wildflowers, "here it comes. Ouch, there goes one of my stems." Just then, a loud noise came from one of the big *Theys*. The little *They* stopped and ran back to the big *They.* Now the trees, flowers, air, and water were confused. The loud noise had made the little *They* stop picking the flowers.

Then the little *Theys* came over to the trees. By now, the trees had no idea what to expect. But what happened was that no branches were broken, no bark was scraped off, no leaves were torn. The little *Theys* only climbed on the big branches.

Soon the big *Theys* called the little *Theys* over to them. They sat down and began to eat. The trees, flowers, water, and air could not understand what the noises coming from the *Theys* meant. If they could have understood, they would have heard:

"Our *environment* is what surrounds us. It is the trees, the flowers, the animals, the water, and the air. We have these things because the people who lived on Earth before us took care of these things and protected them. People will live on Earth after us. And if we do not take care of these things, they will not have them and the Earth will not be the kind of place it is today. That's why we don't throw trash into streams. Throwing trash where it doesn't belong is called *pollution*. Air can be polluted by smoke and different chemicals. Wildflowers are here to be enjoyed and, when they go to seed, they bloom again the next year. That is why we don't trample them down or pick them. Trees also need to be protected. If we damage them and they die, there won't be any wood for humans or animals. In fact, our environment is so important a day is set aside to honor it. That day is Earth Day. Taking care of our environment is not only important, it is the right thing to do."

When the *Theys* finished eating, they gathered up all their trash, put it in a bag, and took it with them as they went away from the glen. The trees, flowers, water, and air had a good day. But tomorrow, good or bad, was another day …

DISCUSSION QUESTIONS

1. Who were the *Theys*? *(Theys are humans.)*

2. What were the noises the *Theys* made? *(Theys made noise by talking.)*

3. Why were the trees, flowers, air, and water afraid of the *Theys?* *(They were afraid because other* Theys *had hurt them.)*

4. How do you think the trees, flowers, water, and air felt when they saw the *Theys* coming? *(They felt afraid.)*

5. How do you think the trees, flowers, water, and air felt when the *Theys* left? *(They felt happy, relieved, etc.)*

6. Why do you think the trees, flowers, water, and air could not count on having only good days? *(Accept any appropriate answers.)*

SUPPLEMENTARY ACTIVITY

1. **Creative Drama:** Divide the students into groups. Assign each group a part of the environment.

    Examples:

    - air
    - water
    - land
    - plants
    - animals
    - sound
    - minerals

    Tell each group to make up a play, using every member of the group, that they can perform for the rest of the class. The play should tell the class about their environmental group and what others can do to help protect it. Tell the students how much time they have to prepare their presentations. When the allotted time has elapsed, have each group perform its play. Conclude the lesson by asking the students to complete the following sentence stem:

    "One thing I can do to help protect my environment is _____."

CORN
NATIVE AMERICAN GREEN CORN FESTIVAL
(ANY TIME FROM MAY THOUGH OCTOBER)

GRADES 3-5

GRATITUDE
RESPECT

WRITTEN BY ARDEN MARTENZ

Arden Martenz is a former teacher and elementary counselor from Pennsylvania.

CORN

It was Julie's birthday. Being 10 was great! Now, at last, she had two numbers in her age. She wouldn't add another number until she was 100, so this was surely a special year. It was sort of like being 13, 18, or 21. Julie's parents had allowed her to pick the place where she wanted to have her birthday celebration and had told her she could invite about 15 of her friends. She selected Kids' Castle, and her parents reserved the main banquet hall. The banquet hall was decorated like a medieval castle and food was served without knives or forks. The waiters were dressed in costume, and being there was just like going back in time. It was going to be a great day!

That was yesterday. Julie's big day has passed. Today, everything is back to normal. Mom is calling her for breakfast and school will start in just a few hours. But Julie doesn't feel like having breakfast or going to school. She just wants to be left alone. Since that isn't an option, she gets out of bed, gets ready for school, and heads toward the kitchen. Nobody pays much attention to Julie until her mother says something and she hardly answers. "What's wrong?" asks Julie's older sister. "Got the day-after-birthday blues?" Julie just gives her a look that says, "Leave me alone."

"After all," thought Julie, "what's the use of talking about it? Nobody wants to hear what's bugging me. And besides, if they did know, they'd just give me a lecture."

Breakfast passed in unusual silence. Then both girls headed for the bus stop and Mom headed for work. At the bus stop, Julie walked over to stand with her best friend, Kara.

"Great party yesterday, Julie," Kara said.

"Thanks," Julie answered in a flat tone of voice.

"Well? Did you get it?" Kara asked excitedly. "I hope so, because I really want to play with it, too."

"No, I didn't get it," answered Julie. "The one thing I asked for! Mom knew I wanted that new videogame more than anything, but did she get it for me? No. She got me other stuff instead. I can't believe she ruined my whole birthday. I waited all day for her to surprise me. I was sure it would be waiting for me when I got home from the party. But no! All that was waiting for me were clothes and a CD that I had asked for."

"What a gyp," said Kara. "I guess you'll have to wait until next year or find some way to earn money to buy the videogame."

The bus arrived and the girls went to school. This school day was about the same as every other day. When it was time for social studies class, Julie took out her book and got ready for another lesson. Her teacher, Mr. Watkins, went over to the closet and began pulling out corn. He had corn husks and ears of corn and he began placing them all around the room. Julie and everybody else thought, "This is weird."

After Mr. Watkins finished setting out the corn, he went to the front of the room and asked the class who understood the meaning of the word *gratitude.* Most of the kids knew that gratitude meant being thankful or grateful for the things you have in life. Then Mr. Watkins asked the class to name some of the things they were grateful for. At first, the students gave the usual answers of family, clothing, food, health, and homes. Then some of the kids began mentioning they were grateful for having a bike, getting to go on a trip, and other things like that. Julie just listened. She had heard all of this before. It seemed like every time it was nearly Thanksgiving, the teacher gave a lesson on being thankful. The only difference was that it was the beginning of October. Thanksgiving was more than a month away.

"Have you ever heard of anyone being grateful for corn?" Mr. Watkins asked.

"How about corn lovers?" asked Billy, hoping the rest of the class would laugh.

"In a way, you're right," answered Mr. Watkins. "Native Americans are so grateful for corn that they have a festival each year when the corn is ready to be harvested. It isn't just one tribe that is grateful for corn, but many different tribes. And because corn can be harvested at different times of the year, the festival can be held any time from May through October."

"Are they also grateful for peas, spinach, and broccoli?" Billy joked again.

"I don't know," answered Mr. Watkins. "But I do know that they are grateful for corn because they used it in so many ways. The corn was eaten, put into soup, and ground into meal for bread and tortillas. Corn was important to the Native Americans and it was a crop that gave them much of the food they needed to survive."

Mr. Watkins walked over to the table and picked up an ear of corn. "Julie," he began, "your birthday was yesterday. Would you have been grateful if you had received an ear of corn?"

Julie didn't know what to say. She had been sitting quietly in class, hoping not to be noticed. She heard what Mr. Watkins was talking about, but her mind really wasn't on it. She was so upset over not having received the videogame that she was having a hard time concentrating on the social studies lesson.

"Me?" she answered.

Kara started to giggle. Just thinking about how unhappy Julie was about not getting a videogame and thinking of how unhappy she would have been with an ear of corn sent Kara into an outburst of laughter. The whole class gave its attention to Kara who, realizing what she had done, immediately became quiet.

"Well, Julie, what do you think?" asked Mr. Watkins.

"I think my first thought would be why would anyone give me an ear of corn? In fact, I might even think it was a joke," answered Julie.

"Why's that?" asked Mr. Watkins.

"Well, corn is not something very many people see as valuable today," answered Julie.

"What you're telling me is that if you receive a gift that you don't think is valuable, you're not grateful," Mr. Watkins responded.

Julie said nothing. There was no way she could defend herself. She just wanted Mr. Watkins to move on to someone else.

"If corn is so insignificant today, why, then, do you suppose the Native Americans still have a Green Corn Festival?" Mr. Watkins asked the class.

"Because they want to party?" Billy joked again.

"There's more to it than that, Billy," Mr. Watkins continued, trying hard to ignore the fact that Billy wanted to disrupt the class. "The Green Corn Festival is like our Thanksgiving. We eat special foods and have a day of celebration on Thanksgiving. We could have a big turkey dinner any time of the year. But Thanksgiving is a symbol. It's a symbol of an event that first took place after people had survived a harsh time. That's what the Green Corn Festival is, too. It's a remembrance of a time when life depended upon a good crop and the harvesting of a good crop meant survival. True, Native Americans can get corn very easily today, but this festival is their way of expressing their gratitude for things they do have and a way of showing respect for the traditions of their people."

Julie was listening now. Being called upon when she didn't expect it was not something she wanted to have repeated. Mr Watkins' last sentence, about being grateful for things you have, had made Julie think. "I really am a klutz. I have been so upset about not getting the videogame that I didn't even think about what I *did* get for my birthday," she said to herself. "If anyone knew how I was feeling, they would think I was really selfish. I'm glad I only told Kara. She understands. At least I *think* she does."

Mr. Watkins said they had heard enough of his talking for awhile and it was time to have the students work together. He told everyone to find a partner. Julie and Kara immediately became partners. Then Mr. Watkins told the students they were going to role-play with their partners a situation in which they are friends and one of them is having a birthday. Julie told Kara that since her birthday had been the day before, she would be the person having the birthday. Then Mr. Watkins said, "The person having the birthday is receiving something made from corn stalks. This is not the gift the person wants. Show how an ungrateful person would act."

Kara pretended to hand Julie a doll made of cornstalks. Julie told Kara that she liked the doll, but she said so a way that let Kara know she was disappointed. The longer the role-play continued, the harder it became for Julie to play the part. She didn't like the way she was acting, and she didn't like the way she was treating Kara.

Then Mr. Watkins told the class to switch roles. This time, Kara would be receiving the present. But this time, the person receiving the gift was to act grateful. The way Kara responded made Julie feel good, even though she knew the present was not really what Kara wanted. Julie had no difficulty seeing the difference between the two reactions. Her reaction had made Kara feel bad, but Kara's reaction had made *her* feel good.

When the role-plays had been completed, the students discussed the differences between the two reactions and summed up the lesson by saying that they had learned to be grateful for what they do have, not ungrateful for what they don't have.

That evening, Julie went into the kitchen. Her mother was preparing dinner. "Mom," said Julie, "I'm not sure if I thanked you for my party yesterday and also for all the nice gifts you gave me. It was really great."

"You *did* thank me Julie, but it's nice to hear it again," answered her mother. "Dinner's ready. Call your sister. And would you please take the corn and put it on the table?"

DISCUSSION QUESTIONS

1. Why was Julie unhappy? *(Julie was unhappy because she didn't get the present she wanted for her birthday.)*

2. How did she show her unhappiness? *(She showed her unhappiness by being grumpy at breakfast and complaining to her friend at the bus stop.)*

3. Why did Mr. Watkins put ears of corn and corn husks around the room? *(He wanted to show the class that something simple and ordinarily taken for granted can be something to be grateful for.)*

4. Why did Billy keep making jokes? *(He wanted the students to notice him.)*

5. Why were the role-plays a good idea? *(They gave the students a chance to understand the difference between gratitude and ingratitude.)*

6. What did Julie learn from the lesson? *(Julie learned that it is important to be grateful for what you have, not ungrateful for what you do not have.)*

7. What do you think Julie thought when her mother served corn for dinner? *(Accept any appropriate answers.)*

SUPPLEMENTARY ACTIVITY

1. **Respect And Gratitude:** Reproduce *Respect And Gratitude* (page 271) for each student. Distribute a copy of the activity sheet and a pencil to each student. Review the directions and tell the students how much time they have to complete the activity. When the allotted time has elapsed, have the students share their answers with the group.

RESPECT AND GRATITUDE

The Native American Green Corn Festival is an example of respect and gratitude. Below is a list of holidays celebrated by Native Americans and others. Write a short sentence explaining how respect and gratitude are also related to these days.

MOTHER'S/FATHER'S DAY

Respect: _____

_____

Gratitude: _____

_____

FOURTH OF JULY

Respect: _____

_____

Gratitude: _____

_____

THANKSGIVING

Respect: _____

_____

Gratitude: _____

_____

VETERAN'S DAY

Respect: _____

_____

Gratitude: _____

_____

MEMORIAL DAY
(LAST MONDAY IN MAY)

GRADES 2-5

PATRIOTISM

WRITTEN BY ARDEN MARTENZ

Arden Martenz is a former teacher and elementary counselor from Pennsylvania.

Introduction: Ask the students if they can state the meaning of *Memorial Day.* Listen to their answers, but do not comment on whether they are right or wrong. Then read the story.

MEMORIAL DAY

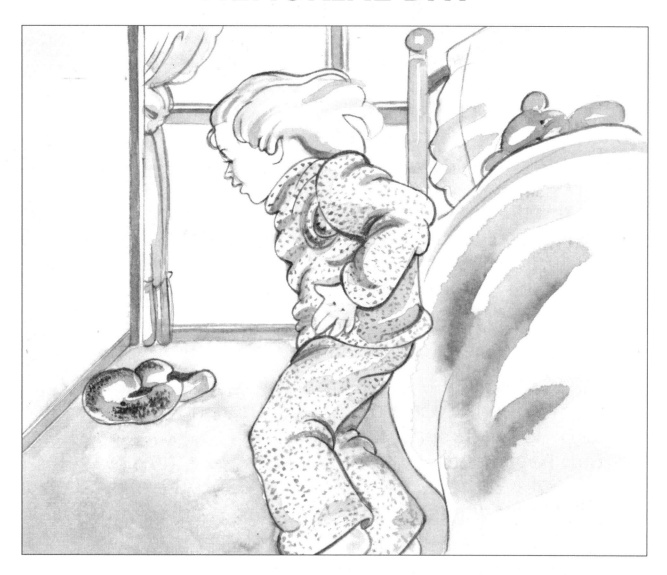

It was going to be a great day! The sun was shining, and Jamie was not staying in bed waiting for her mom to tell her to get up. No way! Not today. It was the day for the family picnic, and Jamie was planning to be ready for it before anyone else. It was the last holiday before summer vacation, the day everyone got together to have fun at the lake. It was called the family picnic, but it was really more than that. It was a gathering of relatives and friends. Jamie's mother was one of the picnic organizers, and she had been planning for weeks what food they would eat and what games they would play. Jamie just wanted everyone to get up and get going.

It seemed like hours before everyone was up and the car was ready to pull out of the driveway. Actually, it had only taken an hour and a half for everyone to get ready, but today was so special that a minute spent waiting seemed like an hour. As Dad drove the van down the street, Jamie looked at all the food Mom had packed and the game equipment loaded behind the back seat. In her mind, Jamie kept saying, "Hurry, hurry! Let's get there!"

As Dad turned down Washington Street, he came to a sudden stop. Jamie looked up. The street was blocked. "Darn!" said Dad. "I forgot. This is the parade route. The street is closed until after the parade passes by."

"Quick! Turn around and go another way," said Jamie. But that was not to be. By the time Dad realized where they were, traffic had lined up behind them. There was no where to go. At least not until the parade had passed the street. Other people, who had probably also forgotten that the street was blocked, began getting out of their cars and moving on foot toward Martin Luther King Boulevard to watch the approaching parade. "We might as well go watch, too," said Mom. "It isn't going to do us any good to just sit in the car."

As Jamie and her parents watched the parade move down the street, Jamie got angrier and angrier. "Why in the world would anyone want to watch a bunch of people, lots of them old people at that, walk down the street carrying flags?" thought Jamie. It seemed like a great waste of time to her, and she told her parents exactly what she thought.

Mom and Dad looked at each other. It was the kind of look parents give each other when their children have said something that truly amazes them. They didn't realize, until that moment, that Jamie had no idea what this day meant. She only knew it was a day to eat good food and have fun.

That night, after Jamie had gone to bed, Mom turned to Dad and said, "You know that trip we've been putting off? The one to Washington, DC? I think it's time we took it. Our daughter seems to be missing an important part of her education, and I don't want her to grow up thinking that holidays are only for fun and food." Dad agreed. And because the family lived near the city, they set aside a weekend in June to drive in and see the sights.

Jamie was excited about the trip. In Washington, she and her parents visited lots of buildings, and Jamie saw things she had only read about and heard about. On their last day in Washington, they drove to the Lincoln Memorial. Then they began to walk. First they came to a place where there were a lot of statues of soldiers. Jamie wanted to go over and run between the statues, but Dad showed her a sign that forbid anyone to go in that area. "That's silly," said Jamie. "Why can't you even walk on the grass by the statues?" That was Dad's cue. Jamie had asked the right question, and now he could begin to explain to her what both he and Mom felt she didn't know.

"You can't walk there, because it's a memorial," he said. "A memorial is something built to remind people of an event. What did you see a little while ago at the Lincoln Memorial?" asked Dad.

"I saw a statue of Abraham Lincoln," answered Jamie.

"What did that remind you of?" her father asked.

"It reminded me of Abraham Lincoln," Jamie answered.

"Yes, that's right. It reminded you of Abraham Lincoln and of everything he did. And that's why these statues are here. They are memorials for the soldiers who fought and died in the Korean War. My father, your grandfather, fought in the Korean War when he was a young man. And do you remember that Grandma June had a husband before she married Grandpa Bill? Well, that man fought and was killed in World War II."

"Why would anyone want to fight in a war?" asked Jamie.

"They don't," said Mom. "Years ago, when World War II started, the government needed lots of men to go to war. The countries of Japan and Germany had declared war on us. Because so many men were needed to fight, the government started a program called *the draft*. This program told men that they were to report to serve in the Army. Some men voluntarily joined the Army, the Navy, the Marines, the Air Force, and the Coast Guard. Some women joined the armed services, too. They weren't drafted, but they wanted to help. So they became nurses and workers behind the lines where the fighting took place. Because so many men were off fighting the war, women went to work in factories to build planes, tanks, and guns to help supply the fighting men with the weapons they needed. The war lasted for years. During all that time, everyone worked together to protect our country."

"Working together was a good thing," said Mom. "But many men and women who go to war do not come back. They leave their families, and their families never see them again. Do you remember seeing the men and women in the parade a few weeks ago?"

"How could I forget it? It made us late for the picnic," said Jamie.

"Yes, it did," said Dad. "But those men and women were marching to honor the men and women who died to protect our country. They were honoring people who paid the highest price of all—their lives—to keep our country free. They died to keep us safe, all we did was be an hour late for a picnic."

Jamie didn't say anything. It didn't seem like there was much she *could* say. She felt very selfish. She, Mom, and Dad then walked over to the Vietnam Memorial, where Jamie saw the names of all the men and women who died fighting in Vietnam. Later, they went to Arlington National Cemetery, where Jamie saw the rows of white headstones marking the final resting places of men and women who had fought in all our country's wars. On the way home, Jamie's parents told her that cemeteries and memorials all over the country honor men and women who fought in America's wars.

Jamie knew that in her own lifetime, men and women had fought in Iraq in Desert Storm and that there had been bombing in Bosnia and Afghanistan. She knew that there wasn't a draft any more and that men and women who *want* to be in the military are the ones who go to war. She also thought that there probably would always be someone somewhere who would start wars, but she knew that she would not forget what she had seen in Washington and what she had learned from her parents. She knew that the next time she sang *The Star Spangled Banner* or *America the Beautiful,* she would remember the parade and how our country is so important that men and women have always been willing to die to save it.

DISCUSSION QUESTIONS

1. What does Memorial Day stand for? *(It honors the men and women who have fought and died for our country.)*

2. Why was Jamie upset by the parade? *(She felt the parade was preventing her from getting to the picnic.)*

3. How did Jamie feel after she learned the meaning of the parade? *(She felt ashamed, understanding of the reason we observe Memorial Day, etc. Accept any other appropriate answers.)*

4. What can someone your age do to show that you care about your country? *(Accept any appropriate answers.)*

FOLLOW-UP ACTIVITIES

1. **Sentence Completion:** Ask each student to complete the following sentence stem aloud:

   "One thing I can do to show I care about my country is _____."

2. **Patriotic Careers:** Tell the students that when they care about our country, they are patriotic. Explain that many people serve our country in their jobs. Have the students name some jobs in which people serve our country (president, other political offices, military personnel, etc.). Allow any career choice the students name as long as they can explain how the person in that career is serving the country. For example, teachers could be said to serve their country because they prepare young people to be future citizens. When the students have finished suggesting careers, distribute art paper and crayons or markers to each student. Have each student draw a picture of a career he/she might like to follow that would serve our country.

CHARACTER-EDUCATION MATERIALS
PUBLISHED BY
MAR∗CO PRODUCTS, INC.

STORYBOOKS

Dabi: The Donkey Who Didn't Want To Be Stubborn
Glenda: A Story About Caring & Cooperation
Ocho: A Story About Character Traits In A Sea Community

GAMES & ACTIVITIES

Character Fun Gamekit
Character Cookies
Character Card Games & Activities
Respect Bingo
Responsibility Bingo
Goals Bingo
Character-Education Bingo (B A-1)
The Student Responsibility Game

PROGRAMS

Character-Building Classroom Guidance (Grades 4-8)
Creatures Of Character (Grades K-5)